A BOOK FOR TH

THE MONEY TREE

A journey beyond the horizon of the knowledge of

CREATING money

CARLA
FREDERICO

A BOOK FOR THE FUTURE GENERATION

THE MONEY TREE

A journey beyond the horizon of the knowledge of

CREATING money

CARLA
FREDERICO

Year of publication: 2019

First impression: 2019

ISBN: 978-0-244-54052-4

Dedication

To my lovely children. Thanks. Without your support and patience, I would never have achieved my dream.

To my mate, friend and confidant. Thanks. Without your support and admirable confidence in me, I would never have started writing.

To my lovely followers. Thanks. For helping me grow and always ready to listen to me or read my books. Also I have to say a word to my haters too... Thank you!

To me for having courage. Thanks. For trusting myself despite all the dismay and inner voices of annihilation.

The Author,
Carla Frederico

Content

Preface

Why do some people achieve success and financial freedom, while others spend their entire lives struggling with money?

You may think that the first group was born in a golden cradle or won the lottery; others may think it's just a matter of luck... But my guess, however, is that what separates these two groups is financial education.

Not only changing mindsets, adopting good financial habits and regularly investing, but also increasing productivity, marketing techniques and entrepreneurship lessons.

Continually learning and developing new skills will surely greatly increase our chances of achieving lasting success in our lives.

To help you out, I decided it would be interesting to talk about the creation of money, its origin and how we got to where we are today, a money-based civilization.

Of course I read many books on the subject that changed my life, and some of them left me with some questions, but none of them gave me the answers I needed to clarify my doubts.

So I decided to write my own book about money for the purpose of leaving something valuable to my children, something that can make their lives easier when they read it and understand the true origin of everything.

Some of the books that opened my mind, among them certainly are the book **Rich Dad, Poor Dad, written by Robert Kiyosaki and Sharon Lechter**, and I can say that it is one of the greatest classics in the financial education literature. This was the first book I read that spoke clearly about financial independence and showed the way for you to stop being an employee and become an investor.

Another great book for me was, **The Secrets of the Millionaire Mind, written by T. Harv Eker**, which is one of the greatest classics of the enrichment mindset, in this book Eker makes comparisons between a poverty-focused mind and a wealth-focused mind, presenting the main mindset changes you need to put into practice if you want to think like a rich person, and from **The Millionaire Lives by Thomas Stanley and William Danko**, in this book I learned the main common habits of the millionaires of first generation who built wealth on their own, not by inheritance.

These books could become a real source of inspiration to start investing more in myself, but none of them gave me the beginning, the real beginning, the origin of money!

In The Tree of Money, I want to get away from these motivational ideas or advice on how to become something, blah, blah, blah, hocus-pocus that many of these books describe, but leave a true idea of what really goes on over the years, where the first exchange system existed. I hope it will be an unforgettable trip and that this book will serve as a basis for future generations.

The author,

Carla Frederico.

Introduction

We do not need an exchange token to do our day to day work. This makes our life easier based on our current model of civilization. We build an empire that depends heavily on currency.

It doesn't have to be that way any more.

If we wanted to, we could end world hunger. Everyone could have food, houses, clothes and all the basic necessities. No one would have to want anything and everyone could work on what they want to work on.

We could do all this today, but what is stopping us now is that we are stuck with the concept of money.

There are people who have spent their lives looking for this, and they don't want it to end now that they are rich. Everyone tries to understand their wealth and their relationship with the currency.

It makes them sacrifice their lives; wasting time doing things they don't like. We could explore new worlds and galaxies. We could experience the universe in a way that expanded our understanding.

Only then will we stop this stupid concept of money.

A concept that makes the vast majority miserable wasting our time doing things we don't want to do.

Things we don't need to do to improve humanity's position in the universe.

The money itself is nothing. It may be a shell, a metal coin, or a piece of paper with a historical image, but the value people place on it has nothing to do with the physical value of money. Money derives its value by being a means of exchange, a unit of measure, and a deposit of wealth.

Money allows people to trade goods and services indirectly, understand the price of goods, and give us a way to save for larger purchases in the future.

Money is valuable only because everyone knows that everyone else will accept it as a form of payment – so in this book I want you to understand how money has evolved and how it is used today.

In writing on the subject, I found several authors who wrote about the origin of money, but in some of them I always see a certain embellishment on the subject.

That is not my idea.

I don't want embellishments on anything; I want it to be as easy as possible and easy to understand, so that future generations can realize that money has certain roots that once understood, we will no longer be slaves to something that has no power.

Except the power we designate.

Chapter 1:

The history and origins of money.

W herever you go, money speaks. And it's been doing this for a long time. Unfortunately, however, money has been muted about its origins. For such a central element of our lives, the ancient roots of money and the reasons for its invention are unclear.

Just as cryptocurrencies such as Bitcoin, Ethereum, Litecoin, etc... multiply into a bunch of digital appearances, researchers are still fighting over how and where the money came to be.

And some draw fascinating parallels among the latest, “buzz worthy cryptocurrencies,” which require only a virtual wallet, a kind of money developed by a Micronesian island community that wouldn't fit in anyone's wallet, pocket, or purse.

When it comes to the origins of money, however, conflict reigns.

Economists have maintained a view of the origins of money for hundreds of years. But an increasing number of anthropologists and archaeologists, maintaining a revisionist view, claim that the standard history of economists is bankrupt.

Economists and revisionists agree that an object defined as money works in four ways: first, it serves as a means of exchanging goods and services.

Currency allows the payment of debts.

It represents a general measure of value, making it possible to price all types of items.

And finally, money can be stored as a wealth reserve.

From there, the two groups separated.

Traditional economists assume that the exchange of goods and services inspired the invention of money.

Anthropologists and archaeologists claim that the early states invented currency as a means of paying off debt.

"Much academic work presupposes that monetary systems have emerged in nation states over the past 200 to 400 years," says sociocultural anthropologist **Daniel Souleles** of the Copenhagen Business School in Frederiksberg.

But financial transactions and debt appear in many much older places in the past.

Recent research from the Americas adds new questions to the debate. These investigations suggest that money appeared independently for different reasons and took different tangible forms in many parts of the world, beginning thousands of years ago.

Since the publication of Adam Smith's The Wealth of Nations in 1776, a consensus among economists states that self-interest business decisions automatically balance supply and demand with little or no need for government involvement.

A natural human tendency to exchange one product for another, (*say pottery for potatoes*), led to the invention of money in former Eurasian states, economists maintain.

This worn-out story gets the wrong money, say anthropologists and archaeologists.

Adam Smith based his" creation myth "on financial systems in ignorance of what really happened in the past," says archaeologist Robert Rosenswig of the University of Albany in New York.

Early governments created money to pay off public works debts and collect taxes, Rosenswig says.

The exchange had nothing to do with it.

Instead, money was born from older credit and debt systems that anthropologists have documented for over a century. In small-scale societies, debts refer to obligations to others.

Among hunter-gatherer and farmer groups, for example, married daughters create debts that are partially paid for with goods known as wedding clothes.

Full reimbursement requires the recipient of the first bride to provide a bride in return.

No money needed.

The revisionists argue that the transition to a new form of cash-friendly debt began at least **5,500 years** in the **agricultural states of Mesopotamia and Egypt**.

In Mesopotamia, the silver shekel – a piece of metal, not a coin – was a basic monetary measure. The rulers decreed that the weight of a silver shekel was equivalent to a bushel of barley.

Shekels of silver, gold and other metals were used in other ancient societies.

Precise shekel weights appear to have varied and are difficult to define.

Farmers were taxed to support real lifestyles and public works.

What farmers and other commoners could not afford on property was recorded as debt in shekels.

Merchants and traders bought property from temple and palace officials on credit.

Mesopotamian-era traders travelling through Eurasia may have used pieces of silver, measured in roughly standardized shekels, to pay for some transactions. But whether these pieces of silver can settle debts is unknown. Coins stamped with animal images or rulers, ensuring the value of the metal, first appeared in the kingdom of **Lydia**, in what is now **Turkey, some 2,600 years ago**.

The first currency units appear in Mesopotamia and Egypt, mainly to calculate debts.

Soon after, cities and states of Greece, Persia, India, and China began attacking their own currencies. From the beginning, the coins financed armies and wars of conquest. In the process, currencies became legal currency for all types of transactions.

Markets were the result of this system, not its cause, argues the revisionists.

David Graeber, an anthropologist at the London School of Economics and Political Science, presented this alternative view in his 2011 book, **Debt: The First 5,000 Years.**

Graeber relied mainly on evidence from African, Asian, and European societies. But his book has inspired a growing line of research into the dark origins of money in the Americas. Many of these researchers gathered to discuss their findings in April, in Washington, DC, at the annual meeting of the Society for American Archaeology.

Some see Graeber's focus on debt as vital to understanding when and how the ancient Mayans and surrounding societies turned commodities such as cocoa beans and woven cotton into coins. But exchange cannot be dismissed as a precursor to perishable payments in the same societies.

For now, there are more questions than answers.

"Debt played a huge role in ancient Central America and Mexico, but it's not clear how the coins emerged there," says anthropological archaeologist Joanne Baron of Bard High School in Newark, N.J.

In the 1500s, the Spanish wrote about observing a thriving system of markets in societies stretching from Mexico to Central America, including the **Aztecs and the Maya.**

Spanish chroniclers described coins, most prominently cocoa beans and cloth, which were widely used to buy goods, pay taxes and debts, calculate monetary values and store household wealth.

An Aztec tribute, or tax collection, the list included jade beads, bird feathers, cocoa and jaguar skins. About 600 years ago, Aztec rulers may have purchased large quantities of cocoa and cotton fabrics from this region to use as coins.

Researchers have long suspected that Mayan markets and traders, as well as various goods used as coins, emerged around 1100 after the fall of kings and city states of classical Mayan civilization.

Evidence now suggests, however, that such perishable forms of money appeared even earlier during the classic Mayan heyday of 250 to 900.

The conversion of several items into legal currency "has taken place in ancient America, not just Europe," says Kathryn Sampeck, an anthropological archaeologist at Illinois State University, in Normal.

Consider a collection of mid-seventh-century murals discovered about a decade ago in a small pyramid in Calakmul, Mexico.

These scenes illustrate market exchanges in a powerful classic Mayan cent-er that controlled a number of satellite sites (SN Online: 4/17/18).

Calakmul's painted pyramid stood in the middle of an open area that included a large market, archaeologists suspect.

Murals on the walls of the pyramid depict people from different social classes, such as indicated by their clothing and jewellery, apparently trading tamales, tobacco and ceramics. Several painted scenes show fabrics of various sizes and colours displayed for exchange.

A painting depicts a woman wearing the simple clothes of a villager offering what is probably a mug of hot chocolate for a man in exchange for tamale pasta.

In the following decades, while Mayan rulers demanded cocoa and textiles as tax payments, a kind of tax collection from the subjects, the two products became currencies with standard values, Baron argued at the archaeology meeting.

A painted vase dating from 691 depicts the earliest known example of textiles and cocoa beans presented as a tribute to a king.

A bag at a king's feet is labelled "3 pik," which the researchers translated as a term for 24,000 cacao beans. After 691, painted pottery and monuments carved elsewhere Classic Mayans increasingly show bags of cocoa beans and bundles of cloth in tribute scenes.

Royal courts probably stored taxes and used them to pay court members and to buy goods from the market, Baron says.

Among the classic Mayans, however, bargaining may have been a direct precursor to cocoa and cloth coins, Baron proposed, in the March Journal of Anthropological Archaeology.

In an analysis of archaeological evidence and reports by Spanish officials, she concludes that people from all walks of life traded fine fabrics in Calakmul markets before kings began collecting fabric tributes.

In Tikal, Calakmul's rival center, specialized weaving tools found in households of all walks of life indicate that the high-end segment began decades or more before the state built markets and collected clothing honours, Baron says.

The collection of tributes from the late 600's to the 700's led to the definition of values for specific sizes and colours of textiles in Calakmul, Tikal and related Mayan sites.

At the same time, increased demand among the Mayan elites for cocoa as a tribute has influenced the emergence of monetary values calculated by cocoa bean counting. "What started as trading items may have become currency for the classic Maya," says Baron.

State Money

Monetary systems probably developed in some populations in southern Mexico and Central America, centuries before the emergence of the classical Mayan civilization proposed by Rosenswig of Albany at the April meeting.

But identifying the birthplace of money in this part of the world is especially tricky, as coins like cocoa and textiles are often not preserved in ancient places, Rosenswig says.

He looks at the main evidence of pottery and murals, as well as the remains of grand palace buildings, public works, and written war accounts. Centralized governments and their need to tax subjects and convert valuable goods into currencies to pay for wars and expensive construction set the stage for Mayan monetary systems, he says.

These types of governmental activities can be documented at archaeological sites.

Cocoa Money

Mayan money of the classical era grew on trees where conditions permitted. Cacao trees flourished in Tabasco and other places with wet river valleys, heavy rainfall and protection from the sun and wind.

Mayan rulers in Calakmul and Tikal collected annual tributes on cocoa beans.

ADAPTED BY E. OTWELL
Source: J. Baron / Economic Anthropology 2018

Consider Izapa, one of a network of Pacific Coast city states in southern Mexico, Guatemala, and El Salvador that stood out approximately 2,800 to 2,100 years ago.

Izapa was situated in a region that contained cocoa, cotton and other resources. Rulers apparently commissioned the construction of temples and other large structures.

Carved monuments show kings committing murders, rituals to justify their rule.

The Izapa kings and surrounding locals demanded large amounts of cocoa, cotton, and two other items that the Mayan Classics may later have used as coins as tribute: shells and salt.

"Coins would have been useful for trade between these nearby kingdoms," says Rosenswig.

The city-states of ancient Meso-America, central Mexico and much of Central America, appear to have created their own monetary systems at the same time as Europeans and Asians began making coins, says anthropological archaeologist Stephen Kowalewski of University of Georgia in Athens. Kowalewski conducted a review of what is known about the size of the states, the political organization, and the markets where goods were exchanged in ancient Greece and Meso-America.

As a growing number of Mayan researchers now believe, Old and New World societies have independently created their own currency and currency systems, he says.

Former American societies circulating perishable coins did not allow some individuals and families to accumulate wealth on the scale of the ancient Greeks, perhaps the best known early miners, Kowalewski said at the archaeology meeting.

In the Greek world, individuals could accumulate and sell land, goods, and slaves as private property. This allowed some Greeks to move from humble beginnings to great wealth. In Meso-America, farming communities have regulated land properties, especially in places with the most fertile soil, Kowalewski said. This has made it harder for non-royals to become rich.

With the flourishing of monetary systems and the accumulation of wealth came slavery.

Not everyone agrees that human beings forced into slavery were treated as units of currency of flesh and blood. But archaeologist Scott Hutson of the University of Kentucky in Lexington argued at the April meeting that before Europeans arrived in Meso-America, business transactions included the use of enslaved people as human currency.

Mayan inscriptions of the classical era, for example, indicate that war captives could be given to kings as tribute.

Some captives were rescued by cocoa and other items considered valuable to Mayan royalty, including the pointed shells.

In central Mexico, Nahua Society, part of the Aztec empire about 500 years ago, farming families sometimes sold their children as slaves to the rich during hard times.

Even when their fortunes improved, Nahua farmers often failed to acquire enough money to buy their children back.

But slavery was a secondary operation for Meso-American rulers, says Kowalewski.

In Greece and other ancient Mediterranean societies, slaves were sold and traded in large numbers. Scholars estimate that slaves made up about half or more of the population of the ancient city-state of Athens, Greece.

Greek slaves extracted silver coins, cultivated the land, and even became highly placed civil servants.

Slavery could have financed the earliest forms of democracy and capitalism in the Mediterranean, says Kowalewski.

However, the ancient Mediterranean and Meso-American states cannot explain everything about the roots of money.

Consider the Chumash Indians, who lived more than 2,000 kilometres north of Meso-American societies in what is now southern California.

Beginning approximately 800 years ago, the Chumash groups began paying debts to their bosses with carved currency from the thick centres of olive-shaped snail shells.

Growing demand for continental goods for a growing number of Chumash living on the Channel Islands off the coast of California may have spurred the invention of shell money.

The Chumash Indians in Southern California used cup-shaped beads carved from snail shells as money that began 800 years ago.

Archaeologist Lynn Gamble of the University of California, Santa Barbara, presented a case for this scenario in April.

"Chumash shell money was made in large quantities on the Channel Islands, which lacked the many resources available on the continent," says Gamble.

Channel Islanders probably spend money in exchange for marriage partners, as well as various goods, such as bird feathers for ritual clothes, she proposes.

The Chumash people used various beads for decoration and commerce long before they were turned into cash in the form of cups, says Gamble. Excavations at Chumash sites have dug up beads made of stone, bone and shells dating back over 8,000 years ago. These accounts were not distributed in large quantities throughout the settlements, as was typical of later accounts used as money, Gamble explains.

Shell money bills came much later, she says.

At that time, heaps of these armband-shaped shell beads appeared in many homes.

The shell money was also scattered in the Chumash cemeteries and placed in graves.

Accounts treated as money did not come until Chumash settlements at that time reached populations of 800 to 1,000 people. Groups of this size needed a default currency to simplify an increasing number of economic exchanges are Gamble's suspicions.

From the beginning of shell money, Chumash commoners have probably always been indebted to bosses and their assistants, adds Gamble.

Late eighteenth-century Spanish accounts describe parties organized by the chiefs of the Chumas, where ordinary people were expected to bring food, shell money, and other valuables to pay for the event and pay tribute to the leaders.

The Chumash people mainly bought and sold goods with their sea currency, which coexisted with long-standing business practices. Once shell money has developed, it has probably been included in debt payments to bosses, Gamble adds.

Whether or not Chumash's money owes more to economic exchanges than mainly to debt, an even bigger puzzle remains.

Some ancient societies, such as the Incas and ancient Andean-based empires, kept meticulous accounting records on all kinds of goods and taxes, but had no money.

Gamble says researchers don't know why money developed in hunter-gatherer society relatively simple of the Chumash people and not, say, in the early 16th century.

In the ancient world, money spoke in some places and never said a word in others.

To understand all this, consider the following examples:

1. James can build fences, but he has no eggs. Joaquim needs a fence to hold his chickens. They meet and James agrees to build a fence for Joaquim in exchange for several dozen eggs. This is a barter trade, the very basic building block of the free economy.

2. Same example, but now Joaquim's chickens are not at the moment. James accepts a note from

Joaquim, promising him eggs, since they later accepted in exchange for fixing the fence.

This note is a proxy instead of eggs. If James changes the note to Santiago, then Santiago can pick up the eggs in exchange for fixing James' stove so he can fry the eggs, and then Joaquim honours him with Santiago.

This note became a trade proxy in the absence of the real thing. This note is a basic voluntary contract, and the banknote is also a currency, as all three people accept it as having value in the business.

The bottom line is that anything can be used as a barter proxy as long as the parties to the barter agree that it has appropriate value.

This all includes personal property and one's work. This is why when two parties agree to exchange labour for barter (*in other words, money!*), It is an agreed exchange of equal value.

But we can't stop here because we all know how this service exchange for money works or even the payment for the time and effort of each job, good or service.

My questions go beyond this idea sold to us!!!

Surely my answers are lost in the minds of so many other people of my generation who come to the same conclusion, we can no longer accept what our parents told us, that money doesn't grow on trees, or that we have to work hard to get it.

Our small portion, surely, these days will be unthinkable for parents to say such outrages to their children as we are in the information age.

Our royal riches are your time and independence.

Money is just an instrument to buy your time.

It is a box for maintaining your financial power until you are prepared and comfortable enough to redistribute or use it. But the whole world has been alienated from real money and has been driven to use a currency – a rogue fraud that is quietly depriving you of your two most important assets.

We are entering, or rather we are already, in an era of economic catastrophe that is the most extreme the world has ever seen.

The turnout that will happen this decade will be the largest in history. In fact, wealth is never lost, it is only misplaced. And that means that on the other side of every disaster there is a moment of opportunity. The good news is that all you have to do to change this crisis in your favour is educate yourself.

The biggest investment you can make in your life is your own improvement and education.

Education about the history of money, finance, currency, how the global economy works, etc...

Education about how the central bank and the stock market can defraud you, and how they can deceive you.

If you find out what's going on and find out how the economic world works, you can put yourself on the appropriate side of this wealth relocation. Winston Churchill once said that:

"The more you look to the past, the more you can see the future."

The way the financial system operates is not fully hidden. It's visible, but it's complicated and people just don't and can't see how it works.

It's very difficult for them to assume that we're involved in such fraud. Besides, some of the things must be hidden, but the truth is slowly coming out.

Mike Maloney believes that all fiat coins in the world *(which are most currencies in the world)* will go to zero – and he is adequately supported by history. It is his goal to run a business that allows people to buy precious metals to protect themselves from this eventuality and uses the profit of this business to fund education on the subject – such as his YouTube documentary *(Hidden secrets of Money).*

I agree that there are some comments in the documentary that may have been qualified a little better, such as the assertion that all fiat currencies depreciate to zero.

This is historically true, but it could have been clearer, it is worth adding that some of these fiduciary currencies were initially supported by "commodities" and successful for many years.

The Roman denari, for example, survived for centuries as a gold coin, until successive emperors decided to lower the coin to amusing wars and public programs *(literally reaching coins with an increasingly high-lying metal content)* until people lost faith in the currency and Rome was no longer able to afford to maintain proper legions for their own defence.

The fall of Rome was a direct result of the degradation of its fiduciary currency.

On the other hand, the Roman Empire of the East *(Byzantine)* continued to market the golden solidus for another 500 years and surpassed the Empire of the West for nearly 700 years.

The question here is, when does a coin collapse?

If the failure is in a local currency, the damage can be contained, but if it occurs in a widely traded currency *(such as Roman solidus)*, empires fall.

It is followed by invasion, suffering, tyranny and the dark ages.

Economic collapse is not usually beautiful.

I personally think anyone who watches this documentary with an open mind and chooses to research more on the subject will be doing him/herself a great favour.

Those who decide to choose holes and lose the underlying warning may not be so happy with the value of their paper dollars in the coming years.

Maloney knows what he's talking about and he did a better job than most by putting it in an easy-to-understand format.

Why do people need money?

There are many theories about the origin of money, partly because money has many functions: it is difficult to accurately date interactions involving currencies of various types, but evidence suggests that they have emerged from gift exchanges and debt payments.

But let's follow the money to see the trade routes!

In the past, as today, no society was completely self-sustaining, and money allowed people to interact with other groups.

People used different forms of currency to mobilize resources, reduce risks, and create alliances and friendships in response to specific social and political conditions.

The abundance and almost universal evidence of the movement of exotic goods over several regions inhabited by independent peoples from hunter-gatherers to shepherds, farmers and inhabitants of cities – points to the importance of the currency as a principle of Union. It's like a common language that everyone can speak.

For example, Americans who lived in the initial formative period dating from 1450 to 500 BC used obsidian, mother-of-pearl bark, iron ore and two types of ceramics as a bargaining chip in the Americas, in one of the first examples of a global trade Successful.

The trade of the Maritime Silk Road, which occurred between 700 AD and 1450, connected Europeans, Asians and Africans in a global trade that was both transformational and fundamental.

Chinese coins were small copper and silver discs with a hole in the center so they could be used on a belt. This coin was issued by Emperor Yongle of the Ming dynasty.

He was interested in political and commercial missions to the lands beyond the ***South China Sea and sent Admiral Zheng He to explore these lands almost 80 years before Vasco da Gama arrived in India from Portugal.***

Archaeological discoveries such as this illustrate Africa's integration into trade interactions in the Indian Ocean.

They also show evidence that cash-based market economies were developing at this time.

On the coast of East Africa, there were local merchants and local Swahili kings who followed Islam and cultivated these external contacts with other merchants in the Indian Ocean.

They wanted to facilitate business, while merchants from the near East and South Asia had their own means of commercial contacts.

The currency was not only a local subject, but also a way to leave a phone card, a signature and a symbolic symbol of connections.

As the history of money showed, the impact of the currency has two edges: it enabled the movement of goods and services, migration and settlement among strangers.

It brought wealth to some while accelerating the development of socio-economic and other distinctions. The same patterns unfold today with the modern relationship between China and Africa, now more intertwined and unequal than when Admiral Zheng He first brought China's coins into a diplomatic gesture, as a symbolic extension of friendship through the distance that separates both.

In our time, cash currency ownership differentiates the rich from the poor, the developer of developing countries, and the global north of the emerging global south.

Money is personal and impersonal, and global inequality today is linked to the formalization of money as a measure of well-being and sustainability of society. Even if the currency continues to evolve in our digital age, its uses today would still be familiar to our predecessors.

Part of the oldest known paper money dates from ancient China, where paper money became common from 960 AD onwards. With the introduction of paper money and non-precious currencies, commodity money has evolved into representative money.

This meant that the money itself no longer needed to be very valuable. The representative money was supported by a promise from the government or the bank to exchange it for a certain amount of silver or gold.

For example, the former British pound project or sterling once secured the rescue of a pound of sterling silver.

Fundamental to all these gradually evolved or fiduciary currencies is belief in the minds of the people.

Governments can dictate the value of a currency to a large extent, but must ensure that the integrity of their currency is maintained, preventing it from circulating too much.

If the currency is based on some precious metal content such as gold or silver, they must maintain that content to prevent currency degradation. For several millennia, the success of national or "fiduciary" currencies depended on their consistency of precious metal content because people saw the value of gold and silver as much more reliable and constant than the "promises" of governments.

During most of the 19th and 20th centuries, most currencies were based on representative money through the use of the gold standard. At first, they were used for exchanges between merchants, but then the government began operating the presses. This resulted in the world's first case of hyperinflation. As a medieval Chinese historian Ma Twan-lin noted, *"Paper should never be money, but only employed as a representative sign of the value existing in metals or products."*

"Sound as a pound" emerged as a key phrase because of British dedication to maintaining the integrity of its currency (the pound) keeping the silver content constant. For several centuries, the British pound has been **"the gold standard"** for most of the world. Gold has been a representation of wealth for many thousands of years and is embedded in most minds as being wealth itself. But that's not particularly useful.

Practical applications of gold are limited and almost 80% is used in ornamentation.

If the total amount of gold extracted was melted into a large cube, it would measure 20 meters on each side. It's attractive, but its rarity and effort to produce it give you value.

Gold is a highly stable trading symbol, not a unit of real wealth.

In most cases of currency devaluation, the percentage of precious metals in currencies was reduced and therefore their value declined over time.

This "inflation" is basically a government tax to deal with urgent financial deficiencies. The flood of gold and silver markets by the Spaniards was a rare case of making metals more abundant and therefore less precious.

This demonstrates that precious metals are more faith than reality and so limited in supply that any currency based on them today would become highly inflated to the point of restricting the expansion of economic activity.

Precious and rare products, which have been highlighted in people's minds for millennia, have proven to be excellent exchange rate stabilizers. But although they dominate wealth, they do not constitute wealth.

CURRENCY "COWRIE SHELL"

As fixed as we are in the west are in the long lasting value of gold and silver, the shell of whelks has been used as a bargaining chip for more people and a larger geographical area than precious metals. The whelk shell is a product of the Indian Ocean (the main source of the Maldives Islands), comes in various sizes and is attractive for both the eye and the tact.

More importantly, it is the only and impossible to fake convincingly. This did not prevent the Chinese from manufacturing their own metal whelks when the supply of the actual reservoirs became smaller.

This underlines the concept that the representation of money plus faith is equal to real money.

The whelk has been used throughout Africa and Asia and has been a trade milestone for so long that its image forms the Chinese pictogram for money. In central Africa, it was still possible to pay taxes in whelks in the early 1900s and buy small items on the market until the 1950s.

Like precious metals, whelks had few practical uses outside of ornamentation, but this and their uniqueness and rarity allowed them to form a practical currency whose use lasted more than 4,000 years and covered the most populous areas in the world.

Their reach was from China to the west and even to North America, as the natives accepted them in the trade of European settlers. Most societies in the world today are used to thinking of gold as a representation of wealth.

THE MONEY TREE

We can look at the shell of whelks as a peculiar sign used by primitive peoples in a time spent.

But at the same time, in a large part of the world, only an idiot would give up a golden whelk.

Both were rare, but at different times in history, in different regions, one had a history of value and the other did not.

Rare products, such as precious metals and whelk shells, are little more than exchange symbols, not real wealth incorporations.

COINS BASED ON CONVENIENCE.

Wheat coin of Egypt

There are very few examples of a practical currency actually having intrinsic value.

Nails and knives were used and most Chinese coins were made of base metals whose intrinsic value constituted most of their nominal value.

But the best example of a commodity-based financial system is the Egyptian use of wheat. For much of their recorded history, the ancient Egyptians used wheat and wheat-based credits as the blood of their complex banking and financial system. Because it is a basic food, wheat contained a high and immediate intrinsic value.

There would always be a market ready for this commodity anywhere and for a wide range of transactions. The Egyptian wheat-based financial system is the closest to an energy-based system in recorded history.

Today, energy has a number of advantages being more ubiquitous in the economy, more easily transferable, measurable and with a wider scale.

But wheat had the most fundamentals, certainly enough to make a financial system run for hundreds and perhaps thousands of years.

There are **no recorded cases of bankruptcies or currency inflation in this period.**

With fiduciary money, financial crises are a regular occurrence.

The Egyptians ambivalent in currency and precious metals used the grain for thousands of years as a gross currency, but the system was elevated to a complete banking network under the Ptolemy's around 330 BC, which shred the grain base to Greek banks.

Grain use was made practical by reliable (relatively) harvesting in the Nile valley, thanks to the annual floods that replenished the soil.

Outside Asia, this kind of consistency was unknown. Wheat as a monetary basis was made practical by the single and reliable cycle of soil and water of the Nile Valley, which eliminated severe inflationary cycles.

This raises the question of whether there were rice-based coins in Asia. Certainly, a wide range of transactions were conducted using rice in feudal Japan and Burma. Japan was clearly closer to establishing a currency and banking system completely based on rice, but not seem to have approached the sophistication of the Egyptian wheat model.

The Egyptian wheat financial system was complete with a central reserve bank and many branches across the country. He presented the first use of credit notes and was not surpassed in sophistication until 2000 years later in 18th-century Europe.

The system could not have reached that level if it were subject to inflation or currency crises. It was its reliability that allowed a high degree of development of such an uncomfortable currency.

Energy is the most reliable and consistent base available and its scalability and ease of transport make it superior to any other commodity as a monetary basis. It is produced and consumed in harmony with economic activity and, therefore, will give a real reflection of the process of wealth creation.

The value of the energy does not change and cannot be lowered. This is not for, let's say fraud will not occur in an energy-based system, but fraud will be easier to identify in the system using scientifically defined units.

Fiat Money

The representative money has now been replaced by fiat currency. **Fiat is the Latin word for "let it be done".**

THE MONEY TREE

Money is now given value by a decree or government decrees. In other words, applicable legal tender laws have been made.

By law, the refusal of "legal" money in favour of some other form of payment is illegal.

The first practical currency outside China, where the weight and purity of the new currency were accepted without question, was stamped in Cappadocia around 2200 BC.

Since then, a lot of coins have come and go. Among the most stable and long-standing with wide acceptance are the Roman solidus, the Italian florin and the British pound sterling *(with 22.5 million silver grains)* that has become the most stable currency and the main source of international funding for several hundred years.

Printed money – notes on paper – coin released and those who make it any link to inherent value in the currency itself.

This made it possible to devalue the currency in much more subtle ways, so that devaluation has become easier and less prone to market surveillance and public outcry.

The results, however, were more extreme in terms of more regular and absolute failure. The press removed several major discipline factors that had previously moderated the actions of desperate or irresponsible governments.

In the millennia since the implementation of printed money, it has served as a method of exchange, not as a representation of the total production of an economy.

Until the last century, a large percentage of the real economy was not monetized, that is, the workforce and much of the material that entered real production was not paid directly.

Little of any subsistence savings or women's work was paid in cash. Trade was not a dominant part of total productive activity.

In the last 50 years in industrialized countries, however, most forms of work have entered the realm of the commercial economy, so that the flow of money is, in fact, widely seen as a complete representation of the human portion of the real process of creation of wealth.

After World War II, the "all-powerful" US dollar supplanted the "unshakable" British pound that had been the foundation of international finance and trade for 200 years and the most stable currency in the world for almost 1200 years. The dollar has been the dominant currency in world history, but it has also had the lowest run of just 60 years for the usual reason of degradation by an overly creative and loose financial system, underwritten by a structural deficit that has no end in sight. *(Or will it have??)*

If the dollar is replaced by another fiat currency of any description, the economic crisis cycle continues. But the perfect coin is there waiting to write the last chapter of the money story.

The Origin of the Dollar ($)

The origin of the "$" money sign is not certain. Many historians trace the "$" money sign for Mexican or Spanish "P" for weights, sinks or pieces of eight. The study of ancient manuscripts shows that the "S" gradually came to be written about the "P" and looks a lot like the "$" mark.

U.S. Money Trivia

On March 10, 1862, the first currency paper in the United States was issued. Denominations at the time were $5, $10 and $20. They became the legal currency under the Law of March 17, 1862. The inclusion of "In God We Trust" throughout the coin was required by law in 1955.

The national motto first appeared on paper money in 1957 in $1 Silver Certificates and throughout the Federal Reserve.

Notes starting with the 1963 series.

Electronic box / ATM

ERMA began as a project for Bank of America in an effort to computerize the banking sector. Magnetic ink character recognition MICR (MICR) was part of Erma.

MICR allowed computers to read special numbers at the bottom of the checks that allowed computerized tracking and accounting of check transactions.

The monetary system broke the system of exchanging real goods on both sides of the transactions and made possible distortions and residual effects.

As long as the coins had a consistent level of precious metals, the distortions were slow, moderate and more easily absorbed. Once the minting could simply be printed, there were no restrictions on abuse and no connection to the real wealth.

The crisis is inevitable and has been frequent. Particularly, as most of the process of creating human wealth becomes monetized.

It is important to remember that printed money represents a claim about real assets in a society, but does not in any way guarantee that actual goods have been produced to meet the complete claims of the printed currency.

Chapter 2:
BUT NOT EVERYTHING IS OK!

"History records that scalpers have used all forms of abuse, intrigue fraud and possible violent means to maintain their control over governments by controlling money and its issuance." President James Madison

Money, money, money, is always there, right?

Wrong.

Obviously, it is issued by the government to facilitate the exchange of things.

Wrong again!

The truth is that most people don't realize that issuing money is essentially a private company and that the privilege of issuing money has been one of the main points of contention throughout history.

Wars were fought and depressions were caused in the battle over who distributes the money; however, most of us are not aware of this, and this is largely due to the fact that the winning side has become and remains a vital and respected member of our global society, having an influence on great aspects of our lives, including our education, our media and our governments.

While we feel powerless in trying to prevent the manipulation of money for private profit purposes at our expense, it is easy to forget that we collectively give money to their value. We have been taught to believe that printed sheets of paper have a special value and, as we know that others also believe it, we are willing to work for all our lives to achieve what we are convinced that others will want.

An honest view of history will show us how poorly used our innocent trust has been.

Let's start our exploitation of money with:

JESUS turns *(many coins)* 33 AD.

Jesus was so upset by the sight of the money changers in the temple, he entered and began to knock down the tables and cast them out with a whip, this being the only time we heard about "him" using force throughout his life. Mystery!!

So what led the pacifist to eventually become so aggressive?

For a long time, Jews were called to pay the temple tax with a special coin called half shekel shekel. It was a half ounce of pure silver, with no image of a pagan emperor. It was for them the only coin acceptable to God.

But as there were only a limited number of these currencies in circulation, scalpers were in a buyer market and, as with anything else missing, they were able to raise the price to what the market would bear.

They made huge profits from the monopoly of these currencies and turned this temple of devotion into a mockery for profit. Jesus saw this as theft of the people and proclaimed the whole organization as being ***"A den of thieves."*** *.

Once money is accepted as a form of exchange, those who produce, lend and manipulate the amount of money and are obviously in a very strong position.

They're the money exchangers.

* *King James NT, Mt 21:13, Mr 11:17, Lu 19:46*

MEDIEVAL ENGLAND *(1000 – 1100 AD)*

Here we find the offer of goldsmiths to keep the gold and silver of other people safe in their coffers and, in return, people leaving with a receipt for what they left there.

These paper receipts soon became popular for trade, as they were less heavy to carry than gold and silver coins.

After a while, the goldsmiths may have noticed that only a small percentage of their depositors arrived to demand their gold at any time.

So skilfully the goldsmiths made gold receipts that didn't even exist, and then lent them to earn interest.

A nod and a wink between them and thus incorporated this practice into the banking system.

They even gave a name to make them seem more acceptable, baptizing the practice of "Fractional Reserve Bank" which means "lending" much more money than deposit assets.

Today, banks can lend at least ten times the amount they actually have, so while you wonder how rich they get charging interest of 11%, are not 11% per year, but actually 110%.

The TALLY STICKS *(1100 – 1854)*

King Henry the First produced polished wooden sticks, with notches cut along an edge to signify the denominations. The bat was then divided into full length so that each piece still had a record of the notches.

The king kept a half as evidence against counterfeiting and then passed the other half to the market, where he would continue to circulate like money.

As only the Tally Sticks were accepted by Henry for the payment of taxes, there was a demand embedded by them, which gave people the confidence to accept them as money.

He could have used anything really, as long as people agreed that he had value, and his willingness to accept these sticks as legal currency made it easy for people to agree. Money is as valuable as people's faith, and without that faith, even today's money is just paper.

The tales system worked very well for 726 years. It was the most successful form of currency in recent history and the British Empire was actually built under the Tally Stick system, but how does the most of us not aware of its existence?

Perhaps the fact that in 1694 the Bank of England in its formation attacked the Tally Stick System gives us a clue why most of us have never heard of them.

They realized that it was money outside the power of the scalpers *(the same thing King Henry intended).* What better way to eliminate the vital faith that people had in this rival currency than pretending that it simply never existed and did not discuss it?

It seems that's what happened when the Bank of England's first shareholder bought its original shares with carved pieces of wood and pulled it out of the system.

You read it correctly, they bought shares.

The Bank of England was created as a private bank through investors buying shares.

Even banks resent nationalization, it is not what at first may seem, as their independent resources multiply incessantly and dividends continue to be produced for the shareholder.

These investors, whose names were kept confidential, were supposed to invest a million and a half pounds sterling, but only three-quarters of a million were received when it was founded in 1694.

It then began to lend many times more than had in reserve, charging interest on the lot. That's not something you could impose on people without preparation. The scalpers needed to create the climate to make the formation of this private concern seem acceptable.

Look how they did it.

With King Henry VI, reaching the laws of usury in the 1500s, scalpers flooded the market with their gold and silver coins becoming richer every minute.

The English Revolution of 1642 was funded by scalpers who supported Oliver Cromwell's successful attempt to purge parliament and kill King Charles.

What followed were 50 years of costly wars.

Costly for those who fight and profitable for those who finance them.

So profitable that it allowed scalpers to take over a square mile of properties still known as the **City of London**, which remains one of the world's top three financial centres today.

The 50 years of war have left England in financial ruin.

Government officials begged for loans, and the proposed deal resulted in a private bank, sanctioned by the government, that could produce money out of nowhere, falsifying a national currency for private gain.

Now politicians had a source from which to borrow all the money they wanted to borrow, and the debt created was guaranteed against public taxes.

You would think someone would have seen this, and realized they could produce their own money and it should not interest, but instead the Bank of England has been used as a model and now almost all nations have a Central Bank with bank reserves fractional at its core.

These central banks have the power to dominate a nation's economy and become the real governing force of nations. What we have here is a fraud of gigantic proportions covering what is really a hidden tax, being collected by private interests.

The country sells bonds to the bank in exchange for the money it cannot raise in taxes. Bonds are paid for money produced from nothing. The government pays interest on the borrowed money, lending more money in the same way. There's no way this debt is paid, it keeps increasing.

If the government found a way to pay off the debt, the result would be that there would be no bonds to get the currency back, then paying the debt would be to kill the currency.

With its formation, the Bank of England soon flooded Britain with money. Without quality control and no insistence on value for money, prices doubled with the money being thrown in all directions.

A company was offering to drain the Red Sea to find Egyptian gold lost as the sea approached Moses.

In 1698, the national debt increased from £1,250,000 to £16 million and raised the taxes at which the debt was secured.

Por mais difícil que seja acreditar, em tempos de agitação econômica, a riqueza raramente é destruída e, em vez disso, muitas vezes é apenas transferida.

And who benefits the most when money is scarce?

You may have guessed.

They're the ones who control what everyone wants, the scalpers. *(Exchange dealer)*

When most people suffer from economic depression, you can be sure that a minority of people keep getting rich.

To date the Bank of England has expressed its determination to avoid the ups and downs of booms and depressions, but there has been nothing but ups and downs, as its formation, with the British pound, is rarely stable.

One thing, however, has been stable and that's the growing fortune of:

THE ROTHSCHILDS *(1743)*

A goldsmith named **Amshall Moses Bower** opened a foreign exchange house in Frankfurt, Germany, in 1743. He placed a Roman eagle on a red shield over the door, prompting people to call **his shop the Red Shield Firm,** pronounced in German as ***"Rothschild".***

His son later changed his name to Rothschild when he inherited the deal.

Lending money to individuals was good and really good, but he soon found it much more lucrative to lend money to governments and kings.

It always involved much larger amounts, always guaranteed by public taxes.

Once he took the hang of things, he turned his attentions to the world by training his 5 children in the art of money creation, before sending them to the world's leading financial centres to create and dominate central banking systems.

J.P. Morgan was regarded by many as the richest man in the world during World War II, but after his death, it turned out that he was only a lieutenant in the ***Rothschild Empire***, owning only **19% of J.P.** Morgan's companies.

"There is only one power in Europe and that's Rothschild." - French commentator of the 19th century*

*Niall Ferguson, THE HOUSE OF ROTHSCHILD, Money's Prophets, 1798-1848

Let's explore a little more about the richest family later, after taking a look at:

THE AMERICAN REVOLUTION *(1764 – 1781)*

In the mid-1700s, Britain was at the height of power, but was also indebted. Since the creation of the Bank of England, they have suffered four expensive wars and total debt was now £140 million *(which already in those days was very much money).*

To make its interest payments to the bank, the British government has established a program to try to increase revenues from its American colonies, an extensive tax program.

There was a shortage of coinage material in the colonies, so they began printing their own paper money, which they called colonial script. This provided a very successful means of exchange and also gave the colonies a sense of identity.

Colonial Script was provided money to help in the exchange of goods. It was debt-free paper money, not supported by gold or silver.

THE MONEY TREE

During a visit to Britain in 1763, the Bank of England asked Benjamin Franklin how he would explain the newly discovered prosperity in the colonies.

Franklin replied, ***"That's simple. In the colonies, we send our own money. It is called Colonial Script. We issue it in proportion appropriate to the demands of trade and industry to make with that*** **products easily pass from producers to consumers. In this way, creating for ourselves our own paper money, we control their purchasing power and have no interest in paying anyone. "**- Benjamin Franklin *

The United States had learned that people's confidence in the currency was all they needed and could be free of loan debts. That would mean being free from the Bank of England.

In response, the world's most powerful independent bank used its influence in the British parliament to push for the passage of the Monetary Act of 1764.

This act made it illegal for the colonies to print their own money and forced them to pay all future taxes to Britain in silver or gold.

*Congressista Charles G. Binderup de Nebraska, despindo os fantasmas de Wall Street.

Here's what Franklin said after that:

"In a year, conditions have reversed so much that the era of prosperity is over, and a depression settled in such a way that the streets of the Colonies were full of unemployed."- Benjamin Franklin

"The colonies willingly would have borne the small tax on tea and other matters if England had not taken their money from the colonies, which generated unemployment and dissatisfaction. The inability of settlers to obtain power to issue their own money permanently from the hands of George III and international bankers was the PRIME reason for the Revolutionary War."

- Autobiography by Benjamin Franklin

At the time the war began on 19 April 1775, much of the gold and silver were taken over by British taxation. They had no choice but to print money to finance the war.

What's interesting here is that Colonial Script was really working so well that it became a threat to the economic system established at the time.

The idea of issuing money as Franklin put "in proportion to trade and industry demands" and not charging interest was causing no problem or inflation.

This, unfortunately, was foreign to the Bank of England, which only sent money to make a profit for the shareholder.

The Bank of North America *(1781-1785)*

If you can't beat them, join them, it might as well have been their argument when arms dealer Robert Morris suggested he be allowed to establish a Bank of England-style central bank in the US in 1781.

Desperate for money, the $400,000 he proposed to deposit, to allow him to borrow often through fractional bank reserves, must have seemed really attractive to the impoverished U.S. government.

Already spending the money that would be borrowed, no one made noise when Robert Morris could not raise the deposit and instead suggested that he could use some gold, which had been borrowed to America from France.

From time to time, he simply used the fractional reserve banking system and, with the growing fortunes of banks, lent himself and his friends the money to buy all the remaining shares. The bank then began lending money multiplied by this new amount to anxious politicians, who were probably too intoxicated with the new "purchasing power" to realize or care about or how it was done.

The coup lasted five years until 1785, with the value of American money falling like a lead balloon. The bank card has not been renewed. The removal of the shareholder with interest did not go unnoticed by the governor.

"The rich will strive to establish their dominance and enslave the rest. They always did. They will always have...

They will have the same effect here as elsewhere, if they do not *(by the power of)* government, keep them in their appropriate spheres.- Governor Morris

The CONSTITUTIONAL CONVENTION OF 1787, 7/2 THE FIRST U.S. BANK (1791-1811)

It worked once; it's going to work again.

It's been six years. There are many hungry new politicians. Let's give it a try. And so it was in 1791, the First Bank of the United States (BUS).

Not only deceptively called to sound official, but also to divert attention from the first royal bank that had been closed. His initials, however, gave a clear indication that Americans were once again being taken for a ride.

And true to its British model, the names of investors have never been revealed.

Having escaped this for the second time, some probably wished that **Amshall Rothschild** had chosen a different time to make his statement at his private central bank in Frankfurt.

"Let me issue and control a nation's money and I don't care who writes the laws." - *Mayer Amschel Rothschild, 1790*

Don't worry, no one was listening, the U.S. government lent $8.2 million from the bank in the first 5 years and prices up 72%. This time, the money changer had learned his lesson; they had secured a twenty-year letter.

The president, who could see an increasing debt, with no chance of paying back, had this to say, **"I wish it would be possible to get a single amendment to our Constitution – taking away from the federal government its power to take out loans."** - Thomas Jefferson, 1798

While the independent press, which had not yet been bought, called the scam "a major fraud, a vulture, a viper and a snake."

As in the first royal bank, the government had been the only depositor to invest in real money, with the rest being raised from loans that investors made to each other, using the magic of the fractional reserve banking system.

When it came time to renew the letter, the bankers were warning you about the bad times ahead if they couldn't get what they wanted.

The letter has not been renewed. Five months later, Britain attacked the United States and began the war of 1812.

However, shortly before, an independent Rothschild company, the Bank of France, was being looked at with suspicion by none other than:

NAPOLEON (1803 – 1825)

He did not trust the bank saying: **"When a government depends on bankers in exchange for money, they and not government leaders control the situation, since the hand they give is above the hand it takes... Money has no homeland; financiers have no patriotism and no decency; your only goal is gain."** - Napoleon Bonaparte, 1815

For both sides of a war to be borrowed money from the same privately owned Central Bank is not uncommon. Nothing generates debt like war.

A nation will ask for any amount to win.

So of course, if the loser is kept until the last drop in a vain hope of winning, then more resources will be used by the winning side before their victory is obtained, more resources will be used, more loans will be withdrawn, more money will be won by bankers; and even more surprising, loans are usually granted on the condition that the winner pay the debts left by the loser. *(This one was not waiting!)*

In 1803, instead of borrowing from the bank, Napoleon sold territory west of Mississippi to the third President of the United States, Thomas Jefferson, for $3 million in gold; a transaction known as the purchase of Louisiana.

Three million dollars richer, Napoleon quickly gathered an army and began to conquer much of Europe.

In each place where he went, Napoleon thought his opposition was funded by the Bank of England, making huge profits as Prussia, Austria and finally Russia were indebted trying to stop it.

Four years later, with Russia's main French army, Nathan Rothschild took on an audacious plan to smuggle a shipment of gold through France to fund an attack by Spain by the Duke of Wellington.

Wellington's attack from the south and other defeats eventually forced Napoleon into exile. However, in 1815 he escaped his ban on Elba, an island off the coast of Italy, and returned to Paris. In

March of that year, Napoleon had equipped an army with the help of money borrowed from the Eubard Banking House of Paris.

With 74,000 French troops led by Napoleon, evaluating 67,000 Britons and other European troops at 200 NE miles from Paris on June 18, 1815, it was difficult to convene.

Back in London, the real potential winner, Nathan Rothschild, was about to put up a bold plan to take control of the British stock market, the bond market and possibly even the Bank of England.

Nathan, knowing that information is power, has put his trusted agent named Rothworth near the battlefield.

As soon as the battle ended, Rothworth quickly returned to London, handing over the news to Rothschild 24 hours before Wellington's messenger.

A victory for Napoleon would have devastated Britain's financial system.

Nathan put himself in his usual place alongside a former pillar in the stock market.

This powerful man was not without observers when he bowed his head and began openly selling a large number of British government bonds.

Reading this to mean that Napoleon must have won, everyone started selling his British bonds as well.

The fund fell off the market until you couldn't deliver them.

Meanwhile, Rothschild began secretly buying all highly devalued bonds in a fraction of what they were worth a few hours earlier. In this way, Nathan Rothschild captured more in an afternoon than napoleon and Wellington's combined forces have captured throughout his life.

The 19th century became known as the Rothschild era when it was estimated that they controlled half the wealth of the world.

As their wealth continues to increase today, they managed to blend into the backdrop, giving the impression that their power has diminished.

They only apply the Rothschild name to a small fraction of the companies they actually control. Some authors claim that the Rothschild's not only took control of the Bank of England, but also supported in 1816 a new Central Bank in America called The Second Bank of the United States, causing enormous problems to the American president.

ANDREW JACKSON (1828 – 1836)

When the U.S. Congress voted to renew the statute of the Second Bank of the United States, Jackson responded by using his veto to prevent the renewal law from being passed.

Your answer gives us an interesting view:

"It is not our own citizens who will receive the reward from our government. More than eight million of the bank's shares are held by foreigners... is there no danger to our freedom and independence in a bank that in its nature has so little to link it to our country?... Control our currency, receive our public money and keep thousands of our citizens on dependency... would be more formidable and dangerous than a military power of the enemy. If the government were to limit itself to equal protection and, as Heaven makes its rains, it rejoiced both in the high swells and lows, the rich and the poor, it would be an unreserved blessing. In the act before me, there seems to be a broad and unnecessary removal from these righteous principles." - Andrew Jackson*

In 1832, Jackson ordered the withdrawal of government deposits from the Second Bank and instead placed them in secure banks.

Second Banks boss Nicholas Biddle was quite sincere about the bank's power and intent when he openly threatened to cause a depression if the bank wasn't chartered again, citing: *"Nothing but widespread suffering will have any effect about Congress... Our only security is in the search for a firm course of firm restraint – and I have no doubt that such a course will eventually lead to the restoration of the currency and the new charter of the bank." - Nicholas Biddle 1836*

By resorting to existing loans and refusing to issue new loans, it caused a massive depression, but in 1836, when the letter was over, the Second Bank stopped working. It was then that he made these two famous statements: **"The Bank is trying to kill me – but I will kill him!" and later "If the American people only understood the injustice of our banking and financial system – there would be a revolution before dawn..."** *- Andrew Jackson*

When asked what he felt was the greatest achievement of his career Andrew Jackson replied without hesitation: **"I killed the bank!"** However, we will see that this was not the end of private financial influence becoming official when we look at...

*Andrew Jackson, veto the Bank Bill, to Senate, (1832)

ABRAHAM LINCOLN AND THE CIVIL WAR *(1861 – 1865)*

With the Central Bank settled, the fractional reserve banking system has moved like a virus through numerous state banks, causing the instability that this form of economy thrives.

When people lose their homes, someone else earns them for a fraction of their value. Depression is good news for the lender; but war causes even more debt and dependence than anything else, so if scalpers couldn't have their Central Bank licensed to print money, a war would have to be.

We can see in this quote from the then Chancellor of Germany that slavery was not the only cause of the American Civil War **"The division of the United States into federations of equal force was decided long before the Civil War by Europe's high financial powers. These bankers feared that the U.S., if they remained a bloc, and as a nation, would reach the economy." and financial**

independence, which would disrupt its financial domination over the world."

- Otto von Bismark chanceler da Alemanha 1876

On April 12, 1861 this economic war began. Predictably, Lincoln, in need of money to fund his war effort, went with his Secretary of the Treasury to New York to apply for the necessary loans.

The scalpers who wanted the Union to fail offered loans of 24% to 36%. Lincoln turned down the offer.

An old friend of Lincoln's, Col. Dick Taylor of Chicago, was tasked with solving the problem of how to finance the war. Their solution is recorded as this: **"Just ask Congress to pass a law authorizing the printing of bills from the legal treasure and pay their soldiers with them and go ahead and win their war with them as well."** - Colonel Dick Taylor

When Lincoln asked if the people of America would accept the notes Taylor said, **"People or anyone else will have no choice in the matter if you do them with full legal course. They will have the full sanction of the government and will be as good as some money; as Congress is given that they express right by the Constitution"** - Colonel Dick Taylor*

Lincoln agreed to try this solution and printed $450 million of the new notes using green ink on his back to distinguish them from other notes.

"The government must create issue and distribute all the currency and credit needed to satisfy the purchasing power of the government and the purchasing power of consumers.

The privilege of creating and issuing money is not only the supreme prerogative of the government, but it is the government's greatest creative opportunity, which, with the adoption of these principles, will be satisfied with the long-felt need for a uniform medium. Taxpayers will save huge sums of interest, discounts and exchanges.

The financing of all public companies, stable government maintenance and orderly progress, and treasury conduct will become a matter of practical administration: the people can and will be provided with a currency as secure as their own government, money will no longer be you and become the servant of mankind. Democracy will rise higher than the power of money." Abraham Lincoln **

From this, we see that the solution worked so well that Lincoln was seriously considering adopting this emergency measure as a permanent policy.

This would have been great for everyone except for the scalpers who quickly realized how dangerous this policy would be for them. They wasted no time expressing their opinion in the London Times. Interestingly, although the article seems to have been designed to discourage this creative financial policy, at its launch we can clearly see the goodness of policies:

"If this mischievous financial policy, which originates in North America, becomes reduced at a fixed price, then this government will provide its own money at no cost. You'll pay your debts and you're running out of debt. You will have all the money you need to continue your trade. He will become prosperous unprecedented in the history of the world. The brains and wealth of all countries will go to North America. This country must be destroyed or destroy every monarchy on the globe. "
- Circular Hazard – London Times 1865

From this extract your plan is to see that it is the advantage provided by the adoption of this policy that poses a threat to those who do not use it. 1863, almost there, Lincoln needed a little more money to win the war and see it in this vulnerable state, and knowing that the president could not get the authority of Congress to issue more greens, the scalpers proposed the Bank's approval National.

Well, act. The act passed.

From this point on, all U.S. monetary supply would be created from the debt of bankers buying U.S.

government bonds and insisting reserves for bank notes. Greenbacks continued in circulation until 1994, but their numbers did not increase, but decreased.

"In several years after the war, the federal government had a heavy surplus. He could not (however) pay his debt; retire his bonds, because that meant there would be no bonds to support national ballots. To pay the debt was to destroy the "money supply." - John Kenneth Galbrath

The U.S. economy has been based on government debt since 1864 and is stuck in this system. Talking about paying the debt without first reforming the banking system is just conversation and a complete impossibility.

That same year, Lincoln had a pleasant surprise. It turns out that the Tsar of Russia, Alexander II, was well aware of the currency coup. The Tsar was refusing to allow them to set up a central bank in Russia.

If Lincoln could limit the power of the money changers and win the war, bankers would not be able to divide America and return it to Britain and France as planned.

The Tsar knew that this delivery would have a cost that would eventually need to be paid back by attacking Russia, clearly in the view of the money changers. The Tsar declared that if France or Britain helped the south, Russia would consider this an act of war. Instead, Britain and France would expect in vain to have the wealth of the colonies returned to them and, as they waited, Lincoln won the civil war. With an election coming the following year, Lincoln himself would wait for renewed public support before reversing the National Bank Law he had been pressured to pass during the war.

Lincoln's opposition to financial control of central banks and a proposal to return to the gold standard is well documented. He certainly would have killed the monopoly of national banks if he hadn't been killed just 41 days after he was re-elected. Scalpers were pushing for a gold standard because gold was scarce and easier to have a monopoly. Much of this was already waiting in their hands and every gold trader was well aware that what they really had could easily be done to look a lot more. Silver would only put and lower the share, so they pressed...

*Lincoln Por Emil Ludwig 1930, contendo uma carta de Lincoln, também reimpressa em Glory to God e The Sucker Democracy, uma coleção manuscrita das Cartas de Charles H. Lanphier, compilada por Charles C. Patton.
**Abraham Lincoln. Senado documento 23, página 91. 1865.

THE RETURN OF THE GOLD STANDARD *(1866 – 1881)*

"Soon after the Civil War, there was considerable talk about the resumption of Lincoln's brief experiment with the constitutional monetary system. If the European institution had not interfered, i would have no doubt that it would become an established institution." W. Cleon Skousen.

Even after his death, the idea that the U.S. would print its own debt-free money sounded alarms across the European banking community. On April 12, 1866, the U.S. Congress passed the Hiring Act, allowing the treasury to invoke and remove some of Lincoln's greenbacks.

With only the banks to gain from it, it's not hard to figure out the origin of this action. To give the American public the false impression that they would be better off under the gold standard, scalpers used the control they had to cause economic instability and panic to the people.

This was quite easy to do, calling on existing loans and refusing to issue new ones, an experienced and proven method of causing depression. They then spread the news through the media that they broadly controlled that the lack of a single gold standard was the cause of the difficulty that followed, while all that time using the Contraction Act to decrease the amount of money in circulation.

Went from $1.8 billion in circulation in 1866, allowing $50.46 per person, to $1.3 billion in 1867, allowing $44.00 per person, to $0.6 billion in 1876, totalling only $14.60 per person and $0.4 billion just ten years later, leaving only $6.67 per person. In a continuously growing population.

Most people believe that economists tell us that recessions and depressions are part of the natural flow, but in fact, the money supply is controlled by a small minority who have always done so and will continue to do so if we allow them.

In 1872, the American public began to feel the squeeze, so that the Bank of England, intrigued in the funds, sent Ernest Seyd, with a lot of money to bribe congress to demonetize silver.

Ernest drafted his own legislation, which entered into law with the passage of the Coinage Law, effectively preventing the minting of silver that year.

Here's what he said about his trip, obviously pleased with himself: *"I went to America in the winter of 1872-73, allowed to guarantee, if I could, the approval of a law demonetizing silver. It was in the interest of those I represented – the governors of the Bank of England – to have it in 1873, the gold coins were the only form of currency."* - Ernest Seyd

Or as explained by Senator Daniel of Virginia, *"In 1872 silver being demonetized in Germany, England and the Netherlands, a capital of 100,000 pounds ($500,000) was raised, Ernest Seyd was sent to this country with this fund as a bond carrier Foreign effect the same object (silver demonetization) ".**

In three years, with 30% of the unemployed in the workforce, the American people began to reassemble the times of money backed by silver and dollars. The U.S. Silver Commission was set up to study the problem and responded by telling the story: "The Dark Ages disaster was caused by falling money and falling prices... Without money, civilization could not have had a start, and with a decrease supply should weaken and, unless relieved, finally perish. In the Christian era, the metallic money of the Roman Empire reached $1,800 million, by the end of the 15th century, had shrunk for less than $200 million, no other transition as disastrous as that of the Roman Empire to the Dark Ages... " - Silver Commission of the United States

Although they could obviously see the problems being caused by the restricted supply of money, this statement did little to help the problem, and in 1877 riots broke out across the country.

The bank's response was to do nothing except to campaign against the idea that dollars should be reissued. The secretary of the American Bankers Association, James Buel, expressed well the attitude of bankers in a letter to other members of the association.

He wrote: "It is advisable to do everything in your power to sustain prominent daily and weekly newspapers, especially the Agricultural and Religious Press; as opposed to the issue of paper money and that you will also deny the sponsorship of all candidates. You are not willing to oppose the government issue of money: to repeal the Law by creating bank notes, or to restore circulation, the issue of government money will be to provide money to people and therefore seriously affect our profits such as bankers and creditors.

Your congressman at once and cheat to support our interest in being able to control the legislation. "
- James Buel American Bankers Association **

What this statement exposes the difference in mentality between an ordinary person and a banker. With a banker, 'less really is more' and each needs an opportunity to explore. James Garfield became president in 1881 with a firm understanding of where the problem was:

"Whoever controls the volume of money in any country is an absolute master of all industry and trade... And when you realize that the whole system is very easily controlled, one way or another, by some powerful men at the top, you won't have to say how periods of inflation and depression originate." - James Garfield 1881

A few weeks after releasing that statement, President Garfield was assassinated. The cry of the streets was for the...

FREE SILVER *(1891 – 1912)*

"Fleecing the flock" is the term that scalpers use for the booms process and depressions that make it possible for them to raver the property at a fraction of its value.

In 1891, a great fleece was being planned. "On September 1, 1894, we will not renew our loans under any consideration. On September 1st, we'll demand our money.

We're going to mortgage and become mortgages in possession. We can take two-thirds of the farms west of Mississippi, and thousands of them east of Mississippi as well, at our own price... Then farmers will become tenants as in England... "- 1891 American Bankers Association, as printed in the Congress Register of April 29, 1913

*[22, 1890) in a speech in Congress to be found in the Congressional Register, page 5128, citing Bankers magazine in August 1873.

** of a circular issued by the Associated Banks authority of New York, Philadelphia and Boston, signed by a James Buel, secretary, sent from 247 Broadway, New York, in 1877, to bankers from all states.

The continued gold pattern made this possible. William Jennings Bryan was the Democratic presidential candidate in 1896, campaigning to bring silver back as a monetary standard. (Silver free)
"We will respond to your demand for a gold standard, telling them, "You should not press the forehead of the work of this crown of thorns, you should not crucify humanity upon a golden cross." - William Jennings Bryan

Of course, scalpers supported his opposition on the Republican side as long as he wanted the gold standard to be maintained. Factory bosses were somehow convinced to tell their workforce that business would be closed if Bryan was elected and everyone would lose their jobs.

The Republicans won by a small margin. Bryan tried again in 1900 and 1908, but lost both times.

He became secretary of state under Wilson in 1912, but was disenchanted and resigned in 1915 under suspicious circumstances related to the sinking of Lusitania, which led America to World War I.

J.P.MORGAN AND THE SHOCK OF 1907

If you want to find out the cause of the 1907 crash, check who benefited is where you would like to look first.

With the stock market crisis causing most overworked banks to fail, in J.P. Morgan steps offering to save the day. People will do strange things when panicked, and this may explain why Morgan was allowed to print $200 million out of nowhere, which he used to sustain things.

Some of the banks with problems, with less than 1% in the reserve, had no choice. You accept this solution or go down.

Even if they found out that their problems had been caused by the same people who now offered the solution, there was not much they could do about it. J.P.Morgan was hailed as a hero.

"This whole problem could be avoided if we appoint a committee of six or seven men like J.P.Morgan to take care of our country's affairs."

But not everyone has been deceived. **"Those who are not in favour of the trust can be expelled from business and people frightened to demand changes in the banking and exchange laws that the Monetary Fund would establish."** - Rep. Charles A. Lindbergh (R-MN)

In addition to making a small number rich to the cost of many, in this case, instability also served the second purpose of encouraging the public to believe that it would be better to live under a Central Bank and a Gold Standard.

Desperate people have little time for logic.

LINCOLN WATCHES

In Washington, the Lincoln statue sitting in his chair is facing a building called the Federal Reserve headquarters.

This institution would not be there if Lincoln's monetary policy had been adopted by the US.

It's not federal and has dubious reservations. The name is an open deception designed to give this private bank the appearance that it is operating in the public interest, when in fact it runs exclusively for private profit for its selected shareholders.

It emerged as the result of one of the smoothest movements in financial history.

On December 23, 1913, the house of representatives The Federal Reserve Law, but was still having difficulty getting her out of the Senate.

Most members of Congress had gone home on holidays, but unfortunately the Senate had not suspended the sentence (without the day), so that they were still technically in session.

There were only three members still present. In a unanimous voice vote of consent, the Federal Reserve Act of 1913 was approved.

No objection was made, possibly because there was no one to object. Charles Lindbergh would have objected: **"The financial system was transferred to... the federal reserve board. This council**

manages the financial system by the authority of... a purely speculative group. The system is private, driven for the sole purpose of obtaining the greatest possible profits. of other people's use of money"- Rep. Charles A. Lindbergh (R-MN)

Louis T. McFadden would have objected: **"We have in this country one of the most corrupt institutions the world has ever known. I refer to the Federal Reserve Council (Fed, the U.S. central bank)... This malevolent institution impoverished... the people of the United States... and practically bankrupted our government. He did this through the corrupt practice of the moneyed vultures that control it**." - Rep. Louis T, McFadden (R-PA)

Barry Goldwater would also have objected: **"Most Americans do not have a real understanding of the functioning of international lenders... Federal Reserve System accounts have never been audited. It operates out of control of Congress and... manipulates the credit of the United States."** - Sen. Barry Goldwater (R-AZ)

Most Americans would oppose it if they knew.

The Federal Reserve is the largest single lender in the United States government, and they are also the people who decide how much the car payments of ordinary people will be, what will be the payments of their homes and whether they have a job or not.

The three people who passed the Federal Reserve Act in 1913 knew exactly what they were doing when they installed this private bank, modelled at the Bank of England and the fact that the Bank of England has been operating independently without opposition since 1694 must have given them a great deal of confidence.

Where there's war, there's money.

War consumes more materials faster than anything else on Earth. In war, expensive equipment does not wear out slowly, they explode. *(It is interesting to note that during the 119-year period from the founding of the Bank of England to Napoleon's defeat at Waterloo, England had been at war for 56 years, while the rest of the time prepared for this, scalpers were getting rich.)*

So there it was, the newly formed Federal Reserve, ready to produce any money that the U.S. government might need rarefied air, with every dollar standing to generate a healthy interest. Nine days after their formation, the founders of the Federal Reserve wished each other a Happy New Year. What good luck could bring 1914?

WORLD WAR I (1914-1918)

The Germans borrowed the money from the German bank Rothschild's, the British bank Rothschild and the French Rothschild's.

American super banker J.P. Morgan was, among other things, also a war material sales agent. Six months after the war, your spending of $10 million a day made him the greatest consumer on the planet.

Rockefeller President and Wilson President Bernard Baruch made about $200 million, while families contributed their children to bloody front lines, but profit wasn't the only cause for involvement. Russia ruined the plan of scalpers to divide America into two, and remained the last major country to not have its own central bank.

However, three years after the start of the war, the entire Russian Royal Family was killed and communism began.

You may find it strange to know that the Russian Revolution was also fuelled with British money.

Capitalist entrepreneurs funding communism?

Author Gary Allen gives his explanation:

"If we understand that socialism is not a wealth sharing program, but in reality it is a method to consolidate and control wealth, then the apparent paradox of super-rich men promoting socialism does not become paradoxically.

Instead, it becomes logical, even the perfect tool of megalomaniacs in search of power. Communism or, more precisely, socialism, is not a movement of the oppressed masses, but of the economic elite." - Gary Allen, Author

W. Cleon Skousen wrote in his book "The Naked Capitalist": "The power of any source tends to create an appetite for additional power... It was almost inevitable that the super-rich one day aspire to control not only their own wealth, but the wealth of the whole world. To achieve this, they were perfectly willing to fuel the ambitions of power-hungry political conspirators who were committed to overthrowing all existing governments and the establishments of a global central dictatorship." - W. Cleon Skousen

Extreme revolutionary groups were controlled by being financed when they were in and cutting, with money sometimes being given to the opposition when they did not. If you find this hard to believe, listen to what the so-called dictator of the new Soviet Union had to say:

"The state doesn't work as we demean. The car doesn't obey. A man is behind the wheel and seems to drive it, but the car does not drive in the desired direction. He moves as the other force desires." - Vladimir Lenin *

Rep. Louis T. McFadden, chairman of the House Banking and Currency Committee during the 1920s-30s, explained this way:

"The course of Russian history was, in fact, greatly affected by the operations of international bankers... The Soviet government received funds from the United States Treasury by the Federal Reserve Board... acting through Chase Bank... England took money from us through the Federal Reserve banks and again lends it to high interest rates for the Soviet government... The Dnieper story dam was built with funds illegally withdrawn from the United States Treasury by the corrupt and rogue Federal Reserve.

Federal Reserve administration and banks. "- Rep. Louis T.McFadden (D-PA) **

Even when communism collapsed in the Soviet Union, Boris Yeltsin revealed that most of the foreign aid was running out, citing: "directly back to the coffers of Western banks in debt service."

* Wurmbrand, "Marx and Satan," p. 49
**Registration of the United States Congress, June 15, 1934

WORLD DOMINATION

With Russia down, scalpers now controlled all major national economies. Like a steam-steamroller and a wolf gathering his backpack, there was only one thing left to do and that was to become global. The first attempt was the proposal of the Paris Peace Conference, after World War I, to establish the League of Nations. Old habits cost to die, and even what they called "the war to end all wars" was not enough to convince nations to dissolve their borders. The league's dead.

If politicians were really being controlled, you'd think at least one would break the ranks and I'd be glad. Many did. One was no less than former New York Mayor John Haylan: "These international bankers and Rockefeller-standard oil interests control most of the country's newspapers and magazines. They use the columns of these newspapers to send in submission or expulsion of civil servants who refuse to comply with the orders of the powerful corrupt." that make up the invisible government....

Theodore Roosevelt's warning has a lot of punctuality today, for the real threat of our republic is this invisible government that, like a giant octopus, extends throughout the city, state and nation... He takes advantage of his long and powerful tentacles, officers, our legislative bodies, our schools, our courts, our newspapers and all agencies created for public protection...

To get out of the mere general, I would like to say that at the head of this octopus are the interests of Rockefeller-Standard Oil and a small group of powerful banking institutions, usually called international bankers. The small circle of powerful international bankers practically manages the United States government for its own selfish purposes.

They virtually control both parties, write political platforms, create party leaders, use the leaders of private organizations, and use all devices to put in the nomination to senior public office only candidates, who are receptive to the dictates of great corrupt, the business... "These international bankers and the interests of Rockefeller-Standard Oil control most of the newspapers and magazines in this country." -John Hylan, Mayor of New York 1927, *

These warnings fell on deaf ears, muffled by the music and excitement of the 1920s. People don't usually complain much in times of prosperity, so scalpers used that boom time they created to neutralize any complaints about their growing control.

*(Former New York Mayor John Haylan, speaking in Chicago and quoted on March 27, 1927, New York Times)

DEPRESSION IN 1929

Stack in front of you the biographies of all the giants of Wall Street, J.P Morgan, Joe Kennedy, J.D Rockefeller, Bernard Baruch, and you'll find that everyone marvels at the way they left the stock market and put their assets on the market.

The gold just before the accident.

They have not mentioned a secret guideline since it was revealed, sent by Federal Reserve father Paul Warburg, warning of collapse and depression. With control of the press and the education system, few Americans are aware that the Fed caused the depression. However, it is a well-known fact among leading economists.

"The Federal Reserve definitely caused the Great Depression by hiring one million currencies in circulation between 1929 and 1933." -Milton Friedman, Nobel Prize-winning economist

"It wasn't accidental. It was a carefully planned occurrence... International bankers sought to bring a condition of despair so they could emerge as rulers of all of us." -Rep. Louis T.McFadden (D-PA)

"I think it can hardly be disputed that Europe's statesmen and financiers are ready to take almost every means to quickly regain the gold stock that Europe has lost to America as a result of World War I." -Rep. Louis T.McFadden (D-PA)

$40 billion somehow disappeared in the accident. He didn't really disappear; he just changed into the hands of the scalpers. That's how Joe Kennedy went from $4 million in 1929 to over $100 million in 1935. During this time, the Fed caused a 33% reduction in the cash supply, causing a deeper depression.

HOW FOOD GROWS MONEY

We've been talking about how the privately owned Federal Reserve can produce money out of nowhere. Let's see how this is done.

1. The purchase of securities is approved by the Federal Open Market Committee.

2. The Fed buys the securities it pays with electronic credits made to the sales bank. These credits are based on nothing.

3. Receiving banks then use these credits as reserves from which they can lend ten times the amount.

To reduce the amount of money in the economy, they simply reverse the process. The Fed sells bonds to the public and money is taken from the buyers' bank to pay for them.

Each million withdrawn reduces banks' loan capacity by 10 million.

The federal bank thus has full control over U.S. currency supply, as each country's central bank does the same way. Bankers, through the magic of the fractional reserve banking system, have the right to create 90% of the money offer. This control ridicules any elected government. Puts so-called leaders behind a toy wheel, like plastic ones, assembled to amuse young children.

Or as the father of the famous aviator Lucky Lindy, Rep. Charles Lindbergh, states, when commenting on the Federal Reserve Act:

"This act establishes the most gigantic trust on earth. When the president signs this law, the government invisible by monetary power will be legalized. People may not know immediately, but the day of trial is only a few years away... The worst legislative crime of the eras is perpetrated by this banking project." - Representative Charles Lindbergh (R-MN)

Or as Woodrow Wilson said: "We have come to be one of the worst governed, one of the most completely controlled governments in the civilized world – no more a government of free opinion, no longer a government by... a majority vote, but a government by the opinion and co-operation of a small group of dominant men. Some of the greatest men in the United States, in the field of trade and manufacturing, are afraid of something.

They know that there is a power somewhere so organized, so subtle, so vigilant, so interconnected, so complete, so penetrating, that they had. I don't speak above your breath when they talk about conviction." - Woodrow Wilson

To clearly establish that this is not a conspiracy theory, but in fact it's how things are controlled, I still quote Charles Lindbergh from the House of Representatives, Lindbergh was well placed to see exactly what was going on at that time and it keeps happening today.

"To make the high prices of all Federal Reserve committees do is lower the re-discount rate..., producing an expansion of credit and a rising stock market; so when... businessmen are adjusted to these conditions, can check... prosperity in the middle of the career, arbitrarily increasing the interest rate."

It can cause the pendulum of a rising market and drop smoothly back and forth by small changes in the discount rate, or cause violent fluctuations by greater rate variation, and in any case will have inside information as to the financial conditions and early knowledge, of the change to come, whether up or down.

This is the strangest and most dangerous advantage ever put into the hands of a special privileged class of any government that ever existed. The system is private, driven for the sole purpose of obtaining the greatest possible profits from other people's use of money.

"They know beforehand when they create panics to their advantage. They also know when to stop panic. Inflation and deflation work equally well for them when they control finances... " - Representative Charles Lindbergh (R-MN)

ADOLF'S BANKERS

Most of everyone will be aware of Hitler's rise to power. What they probably don't know is that it was almost completely funded by money taken from the privately owned U.S. Federal Reserve.

"After World War I, Germany fell into the hands of international bankers. Those bankers bought it and now own it, close, stock and put it in barrels. They bought their industries, they have mortgages on their soil, they control their production, and they control all their public services."

The German international bankers subsidized Germany's current government and also provided all the dollars of the money Adolf Hitler used in his lavish campaign to create threat to bruening's government. When Bruening fails to obey the orders of German international bankers, Hitler is brought in to scare the Germans into submission... Through the Federal Reserve Board, more than $30 billion of American money was injected in Germany. Have you all heard of the expenses that happened in Germany???

Modernist dwellings, their large planetariums, their gyms, their pools, their beautiful public roads, their perfect factories.

All this was done with our money.

All this was given to Germany through the Federal Reserve Board. The Federal Reserve Board injected so many billions of dollars into Germany that they dare not name the total." - Congressman Louis T.McFadden (D-PA), who served 12 years as chairman of the Banking and Currency Committee.

FORT KNOX

In 1933, new President Franklin D. Roosevelt signed a bill requiring all American people to surrender all their gold at a basic rate.

Except for rare coins.

He left the project claiming not to have read it and his Treasury Secretary claimed this was "what experts wanted."

Bought at the price of banana with money produced out of nowhere by the Federal Reserve, gold was melted and stacked in the newly built gold deposit called Fort Knox. After collected in 1935, the price of gold rose from $20.66 to $35 per ounce, but only non-American gold qualified to be sold. This meant that those who had avoided the accident, investing in gold they had sent to London, could now almost double their money, while the rest of America starved.

But that's not all personal, oh no, there's even more... much more.

At the end of World War II, Fort Knox held 70% of the world's gold, but over the years it was sold to European scalpers, while a public audit of Fort Knox's reserves was repeatedly denied.

Rumours spread about the lack of gold.

"Allegations of lack of gold from our Fort Knox coffers are being widely discussed in European circles. But what is intriguing is that the administration is not hastily demonstrating conclusively that there is no cause for concern for our gold treasure – if it is indeed in a position to do so. " - Edith Roosevelt

Finally, in 1981, President Ronald Reagan was persuaded to take a look at Fort Knox with the intention of reintroducing the Gold Standard. He named a group called The Gold Commission.

They found that the U.S. Treasury had no gold. All of Fort Knox's remaining gold is now being held as collateral by the Federal Reserve against the national debt. Using credits made out of nowhere.

The Fed had stolen the largest treasure trove of gold on earth.

World War II (1939-1945)

World War II saw U.S. debt rise by 598%, while Japan's debt rose by 1,348%, France by 583% and Canada by 417%. When you read this, what's your first impression? Do you automatically think this is bad or is that good? Most of us feel a well-programmed sense of despair when we hear figures like this, but remember: for scalpers, that's music to your ears. With the war hot, the cold war began, the arms race causing more and more loans. Now, scalpers could really focus on global domination.

First step, the European Monetary Union and NAFTA.

Second step, centralize the global economy through the World Bank, the IMF and GATT (now the WTO).

THE WORLD CENTRAL BANK (1948 – Present)

In Washington, the headquarters of the World Bank and the IMF (International Monetary Fund) face each other on the same street. What are these organizations and who controls them? To find out, we need to look back right after the First World War.

At this point, scalpers were trying to consolidate central banks under the guise of pacification. To prevent future wars, they proposed the formation of a global central bank called the Bank of International Compensation, a world court called the World Court of The Hague, and world law executive called the League of Nations.

In his 1966 book entitled Tragedy and Hope, President Clinton's mentor Carroll Quigley writes of it: ***"The powers of financial capitalism had [a] far-reaching plan, nothing less than creating a global system of financial control at hand capable of dominating the political system of each country and the economy of the world as a whole. This***

system should be controlled feudally by the world's central banks, acting together, by secret agreements, meeting at frequent meetings and conferences.

The culmination of the system would be bank for international settlements in Basel, Switzerland, a private bank owned and controlled by the world's central banks, which were private companies. Each central bank... He sought to dominate his government for his ability to control treasury loans, manipulate foreign exchanges, influence the level of economic activity in the country and influence cooperative politicians for subsequent economic rewards in the business world. "- Carroll Quigley, professor at Georgetown University

They got 2 out of three. The League of Nations failed largely due to the suspicions of the people and while the opposition focused on it, the other two proposals escaped. It would take another war to wear public resistance. Wall Street invested heavily to rebuild Germany, as Chase bank had supported the Russian revolution.

Now Chase merged with Manhattan Bank of Warburg to form the Manhattan Chase, which would later merge with The Chemical Bank to become Wall Street's largest bank.

In 1944, the U.S. approved its full stake in the IMF and the World Bank. In 1945, the second

League of Nations was approved under the new name "The United Nations". The war dissolved the entire opposition. The methods used in the National Banking Act of 1864 and the Federal Reserve Act of 1913 were now simply used on a global scale. The Federal Reserve Act, which allows the creation of Federal Reserve notes, is mirrored by the IMF authority to produce money, called Special Drawing Rights (SDR's). The IMF is estimated to have produced $30 billion in SDRs so far.

In the United States, SDRs are already accepted as legal money, and all other member countries are being pressured to do the same. With the SDR being partially backed by gold, a world gold standard sneaks through the back door, which has no objection from scalpers who now hold two-thirds of world gold and can use it to structure the world economy, to its advantage Additional.

We moved from the fraud of goldsmiths reproduced on a national scale by the Bank of England and the Federal Reserve, to a global level with the IMF and the World Bank.

Unless together we stop giving these exchange units their power for our collective faith and in them, the future will probably see the Intergalactic Bank and the Reserve of the Federation of Planets installed in the same way. (if it doesn't exist already, just saying...)

This radical transfer of power occurred without absolutely any mandate from the people.

Nations borrow the international monetary fund's special looting right to pay interest on their growing debts. With these SDRs produced free of charge, the IMF charges more interest.

This, unlike bold claims, does not alleviate poverty or promote any development. It only creates a steady flow of wealth, from borrowing-taking countries to the scalpers who now control the IMF and the World Bank.

The permanent debt of third world countries is constantly being increased to provide temporary poverty relief caused by previous loans.

These repayments already exceed the amount of new loans. By 1992, Africa's debt had reached $290 billion, which equates to two and a half years higher than it was in 1980.

A noble attempt to pay this has caused increased infant mortality and unemployment, as well as deteriorating schools and general health and wellness problems. As world resources continue to be sucked into this insatiable black hole of greed, if allowed to continue, the whole world will have a similar fate.

As a prominent Brazilian politician, Luis Ignacio Silva once said: ***"Without being radical or overly daring, I will say that World War III has already begun – a silent war, not so less sinister. This war is overthrowing Brazil, Latin America and virtually the entire Third World. Instead of soldiers dying there are children, instead of millions of wounded there are millions of unemployed, instead of destroying bridges there is the destruction of factories, schools, hospitals and entire economies...***

It's a United States war.

Against the Latin American continent and the Third World, it is a war against external debt, which has as main arms interest, a weapon more deadly than the atomic bomb, more destructive than a laser beam.

If a group or organization had used their hard earned money to help these developing nations, we could sympathize with the need for a real effort to pay off these loans.

But the money used was created from fractional bank reserves.

The money lent to the Third World came from the 90% that banks allow themselves to lend themselves in the 10% they actually held.

It didn't exist, it was created from scratch and now people are suffering and dying in an effort to pay it back.

That went beyond smart financing, it's a sales murder, and it's time for us to stop. Can we!" - Luis Ignacio Silva, at the Havana Debt Conference in August 1985, quoted by Susan George, A Fate Worse Than Death, p. 238

This machine has no one to stop it, because the system was made to dazzle all those who enter it, even the best human beings, with the best of intentions, in the end, came out as corrupt as all others. Understanding history and educating yourself on the fundamentals of the economy will prepare you for the future and help you achieve true prosperity.

Cycles of Wealth

"It's good that the people of the nation don't understand our banking and monetary system, because if they did, I believe there would be a revolution before tomorrow morning." - Henry Ford, founder of Ford Motor Co.

When most people deposit a pay check or make an INDIVIDUAL retirement account, they see the money entering your account. But I see something different now. I see billions of working people filling their savings and retirement accounts with currency.

The currency is created by the network of currency houses, central banks and governments that make up the global monetary system.

Almost every transaction around the world involves a currency exchange of some kind. Dollars, Euros, Yen, Pounds whatever his name.

That's why most people believe that currency is money. But that's not true. In fact, all the coins in today's world are fiduciary.

Fiat is just a fancy word that means a coin is officially printed and accepted by a government. It's like a symbol of authenticity. Much like the brilliant stickers of "genuine merchandise", the brand new Major League baseball caps, unless someday they can be worth more.

Fiduciary currencies only have value because the governments that publish them say yes. Of course, there is an underlying demand for fiat currency because governments require citizens and businesses to pay taxes to them in their official currency.

So, almost everyone needs this.

But in addition, fiduciary currencies have no intrinsic value. They're official sheets of paper.

Technically, they're useless. Fiat coins cannot be exchanged for gold or silver. And because of that, all fiduciary coins lose value.

But it hasn't always been that way; we can see it in the past.

Which may be why most people believe that their currency, the economy of their lives, has value... But before our All-Fiat monetary system... Once upon a time, the U.S. dollar and many other currencies derived from its value of gold stored in national treasures. Indeed, each currency unit it was a kind of IOU for the holder, meaning it was supported by a similar amount of gold.

As Mike* described in his book, Guide to Investing in Gold and Silver, before the Federal Reserve was created, every U.S. Treasury note (paper dollar) was fully guaranteed by gold or silver. When the Federal Reserve Act was approved in 1913, the amount of gold in each dollar was reduced to only 40% of the face value of the existing currency. Indeed, this allowed the U.S. government to increase the amount of currency it could create and spend by 60%, enabling loss-making spending for World War I and the consequent increase in currency supply.

Then, in 1934, the U.S. government devalued the dollar by 41% by raising the price of gold from $20.67 per ounce – the price set in 1834 – to $35.

This revaluation of the dollar raised the value of gold held at the U.S. Treasury, so it once again corresponded to the total value of the monetary base, or all dollars then in circulation. Indeed, the US dollar was once again fully supported by gold.

Under Bretton woods' system, the U.S. dollar was designated as the world's reserve currency. Most other countries tied their currencies to the dollar, and the U.S. in return agreed to redeem U.S. dollars in gold at a rate of $35. Under Bretton Woods, the world was essentially in the Dollar Standard.

But it turned out that Bretton Woods' system was not up to the complexities of a modern global economy. The currency offer was once again inflated to fund the social programs of World War II, Korea, Vietnam and President Lyndon B. Johnson. The United States' foreign policy increasingly meant spending a lot of money in other countries on foreign aid, military and defence spending, as well as investment and international trade. As a result, many more dollars flowed into the treasures of other nations, let alone capital flowed back into the U.S. Treasury, resulting in imbalances.

From the 1950s, the U.S. government and the Fed have undertaken a series of free market interventions aimed at balancing the U.S. monetary system.

As is always the case, ultimately, where the authorities interfere with the functioning of the free market, because all actions taken are unintended and generally destructive consequences.

Long-term interest rates kept artificially low encouraged foreign loans and discouraged domestic investment. French President Charles de Gaulle opposed the use of the dollar as the world's reserve currency. Then France began to buy dollars and exchange them in gold, seriously depleting the gold supply at the U.S. Treasury.

As described by History Central.com:

"By the end of the 1960s, it was clear that the evils that afflicted the international monetary system and the US dollar would have to be treated on a basic level.

The Kennedy and Johnson administrations applied solutions to the growing balance of payments crisis, which, at best, were jobs, patches, postponements of the inevitable.

The balance sheet of payments was unbalanced, the dollar was overvalued. Speed was increasing, and the United States could do little to restore economic order without compromising the main aspects of domestic and foreign policy."

In the end, the United States failed to fulfil its commitment to the rest of the world under Bretton woods' system and keep the U.S. dollar tied to gold at a rate of $35 per ounce.

The main point is that Bretton Woods did not allow the United States "flexibility" - the ability to create as much money as needed – to fund its national and foreign political goals.

In 1971, the United States was basically bankrupt; they didn't have enough gold in the Treasury to redeem all the dollars in circulation. (So far we already know why.)

That year, President Nixon cut the bond between the U.S. dollar and gold. With its act, in fact, all the currencies in the world – thanks to the status of the dollar as the world's reserve currency – have become fiat currency.

A currency is fiat if it is not supported by gold or any other asset. The only thing that supports fiduciary currency is faith. As Michael Maloney wrote in his book:

"A decree is an arbitrary decree, order or pronouncement given by a person, group or body with absolute authority to apply it. A currency that derives its value from the declaratory decree or an authoritarian order of the government is, by definition, a fiduciary currency."

Now free of American and global monetary policy, the free market offered the price of gold up to $850 per ounce in 1980.

At that time, the value of gold held at the U.S. Treasury exceeded the total value of the monetary base – the total of dollars in circulation – plus all existing dollars in the form of pending revolving credit.

We measure the amount of currency in circulation by adding the number of dollars in circulation and bank reserves (monetary basis) to the total of dollars represented by the rotating credit in circulation, which is mainly in the form of credit card balances not Paid.

We include credit card purchases because when you charge a purchase on your credit card in effect, a new currency is created in the amount of your charge. This new currency remains in circulation until you pay your balance on your credit card.

More consumers use credit cards as a means of trading instead of money, and so the digital equivalent of money should be included in our modern monetary system.

Here is the unstable Foundation of our modern monetary system.

In all likelihood, 99% of the world's population does not understand the ground on which the global monetary system – our fiduciary currency system –

is based. Many people still believe that the U.S. dollar is backed by gold in the vault in Fort Knox.

Most have no idea that the only thing that supports all the currencies in the world today (including the US dollar) is the debt and solemn promise of every government to tax its citizens in the future to pay that debt. In the United States, this promise is called the Treasury's title.

"If the government abstains from regulation (taxation), the uselessness of money becomes apparent and fraud can no longer be concealed." - John Maynard Keynes on Consequences of Peace

Meanwhile, currency wars continue, while nations continually devalue their own currencies to keep them low against the dollar. Every country wants a weaker currency because it helps its exports and GDP figures.

By weakening their currencies, governments are able to keep their goods prices low, making them more attractive to foreign buyers.

The devaluation of the dollar by the United States by creating currency actually forces other nations to devalue their currencies as well.

It's all upside down, but it's a political death to have a national currency strengthened in a world of fiduciary currency degradation.

But currency wars are not free consequences. Check out what Belgian economist Robert Triffin describes about the growing international conflict over monetary policy...

"Consider, for example, the tension between demand from emerging economies for reserves and their fear that the main reserve currency, the dollar, could lose value – a dilemma first observed in 1947 by Robert Triffin, a Belgian economist. When the world relies on a single reserve currency, Triffin argued, the country of origin of the currency must issue many assets (usually government bonds) to lubricate global trade and meet demand for reserves.

But the more bonds it emits, the less likely you will be to honour your debts. In the end, the insatiable demand of the world for the "risk-free" booking feature will make this asset anything other than risk-free.

As an illustration of modern headquarters by dollars, the IMF estimates that with the actual accumulation rate, global reserves would rise from 60% of U.S. GDP today to 200% by 2020 and nearly 700% by 2035. "- The Economist

The world economy is on the verge of a deflationary spiral. Governments and central banks are taking desperate action, flooding the global currency economy in the form of stimulus packages, bailouts, loss-making spending, cheap credit and fees, all in an effort to ward off deflation. CAUTION!! The problem is that as growth stagnates and declines, debt payments will become impossible.

The strength of the U.S. economy and its financial situation are more unstable than at any other time in history.

The national debt is now $19.4 trillion, with total U.S. debt above $66 trillion.

Add unfunded liabilities such as Social Security and Medicare, and the total reaches an incredible $103 trillion.

These numbers are neither sustainable nor refundable!

Is gold the center of wealth transfer?

Although we do not have empirical data before the establishment of the U.S. Federal Reserve, it seems that the free market has periodically revalued gold – increasing its value to account for excess currency in circulation – time after time, in the last 2,400 years.

This lesson in history tells us that the free market will increase the price of gold until the value of gold is once again in balance with the value of the currency in circulation.

And with a world economy more interconnected than ever before, and with all the world's now fictitious currencies, we can expect the free market to boost enough gold prices to account for the entire currency now in circulation around the world.

If that happens, it will not be unusual just the story repeating itself.

In the long run, inflation is inevitable as governments and central banks continue to implement their inflationary policies to reduce the cost of debt, prevent deflation and stimulate their economies.

The more the coin fluctuates, the higher the price of gold and silver. That's because, throughout history, every time a nation has degraded and finally destroyed its currency, the free market chose gold and silver as the ideal money.

But the massive expansion of currency supply around the world has created favourable conditions for a huge currency crisis. Ultimately, gold will not only benefit from the massive expansion of currency supply, but will also benefit from the global monetary crisis lurking.

During these future crises, it is almost certain that gold and silver holders will be the beneficiaries of the wealth transfer that will occur as the whole world rushes to safe haven assets.

The next race for precious metals will be a completely different kind of bullish market, because not only will you get buyers in search of opportunity, but will also panic with investors trying to regain their wealth. The next monetary crisis will offer a once-in-a-lifetime opportunity that will benefit from fear and greed at the same time.

Actually, I think it's going to be the biggest opportunity in history.

Gold and silver that increase in value against fiduciary coins are inevitable.

As Mike stated in his book, ***"it's as sure as sunrise."*** It's not going to be pretty when that happens.

I'm not saying it's the end of the world or the Day of Judgment. All you can do is stay informed about what really is going on and take the necessary actions.

And if that happens, and I believe that's going to happen, no matter what we do, because it's just all that energy that has accumulated being released. When that happens, it won't be good for most people.

It's only going to be good for some. These are the people who have gold and silver.

I also believe this is the greatest opportunity in the history of humanity that is taking place now. This decade will be completely different from anything any of us have known. There will be global changes with the financial system, with all currencies. This occurred in small bubbles.

It occurred in specific countries, one at a time, and there was always another place that people could manage to protect their purchasing power and protect their wealth.

Even during hyperinflation in Weimar Germany or Zimbabwe, a few years ago you would have your wealth in US dollars.

Well, if all the currencies on the planet are failing, that means it's not necessarily failing, but if they're all sick at the same time, they're suffering from huge inflation or a lack of confidence in which I believe it will happen, lack of trust and lack of faith.

At this point, there is no other place except precious metals and therefore there has never been a simultaneous global global demand.

This is a new phenomenon that is happening now. This will be the greatest transfer of wealth in the history of mankind. So it's the greatest opportunity in the history of mankind.

My mission is to try to inform as much of the middle class as possible of this planet before the major economic changes happen. It's all back because we're in a bigger bubble; remember it was 18 years in the 1900s.

Today all Western currencies are only backed by debt. It is absolutely essential to understand the implications of this fact: the support that 100 years ago was made by gold was replaced by a promise of payment on a piece of paper.

*Mike Maloney- Guide to Invest in Gold & Silver.

Unlike gold, a promise of payment can go, poof, if the debtor goes bankrupt. Like a couple of balances with money on one side and gold on the other, today we have money on one side and debt on the other.

If this debt goes wrong, because the debtor goes bankrupt in today's system, money also loses its value, since it is not supported by anything when the promise of payment becomes useless.

This is one of the main reasons for all bailouts of large banks or even from entire countries.

If a small business goes bankrupt and its promise to pay its debt becomes useless, the bank that granted the loan to that company will have to void this money as a financial loss on its balance sheet.

If the same thing happens to a large bank or even with an entire country, this can result in a chain reaction that causes the implosion of the entire monetary system, rendering all the money in the system useless. If a country goes bankrupt – for not being able to pay its regular expenses – this is called national bankruptcy.

Chapter 3:

Creating money in a debt-based monetary system.

As I have just described, the money is inseparably linked to debt in the existing system. When the question "where did money originate" or how it is "created" there is a clear answer:

Money can only be "created" when someone signs a debt obligation – in other words, a promise to pay the loan.

Two scenarios should be differentiated:

A) If a company issues a loan, it can borrow money from individuals who already have that money. In this case, no new money is created, but money just changes hands.

B) The money is "created" by central banks (*such as the Federal Reserve Bank in America or the ECB in Europe*). If a government issues a government title, the central bank can "buy" that title.

Unlike the process described above, the central bank does not need to have money to pay the government. Because a central bank has a monopoly on "creating money from nothing," it can simply "create" money equivalent to the value of the title. The government's title is then seen as collateral for newly created money and the government receives money from the central bank.

During the financial crisis in recent years, central banks (especially the U.S. EDF) have also accepted other guarantees, as well as government bonds, to print new amounts in return. An example of lower assurance that has been accepted is what became known as "sub-prime" loans granted to highly indebted homeowners.

These "sub-prime" loans were packaged in large quantities by major banks and then delivered to the EDF in exchange for money "created from nothing."

The total sum of new money that the EDF has created since 2007 is unknown, as in 2006 the EDF decided it would no longer publish the amount of money in circulation - a number also known as "M3".

Even though this cover-up tactic obscured the exact amount of money created in December 2010, the EDF was forced by a U.S. court to disclose data related to its bailout programs to major banks.

This revelation revealed that within the "TAF" rescue program, $3.3 trillion ($1.25 trillion) was created for "sub-prime" loans. In addition, for the "TAF" program, an additional program called "PDCF" was issued to provide access to additional loans to large banks.

By adding the available figures for all the different redemption programs, we get the following amount of money for these banks: Citigroup $2.2 trillion, Merrill Lynch $2.1 trillion, Morgan Stanley $2.0 trillion, Bank of America $1.1 trillion, Bear Stearns $960 billion and Goldman Sachs $620 billion.

The total sum of the bailout money is in the double-digit range of the trillion dollars – an outrageous figure compared, for example, to Germany's national debt, which stood at 2.042 trillion euros in March 2012.

The term "quantitative easing" was used very recently in the mainstream media when it referred to the latest fed measure. Even though the term may sound attractive, what it represents is another EDF program to buy government bonds and, in return, create new money out of nowhere. In the first steps, $600 billion was agreed, but the next steps are expected.

An article in the German magazine Spiegel of 22 May 2011 shows that the European Central Bank also accepted guarantees with questionable value.

The guarantee in question is "several hundred billion euros". In a Spiegel article published on 6 June 2011, the aforementioned guarantee is equivalent to 840 billion euros, of which 360 billion are labelled "non-marketable".

These amounts do not yet include government bonds from Greece, Spain, Portugal and Ireland that the ECB has bought in recent months. Between May 2010 and early October 2011, the ECB bought government bonds for €160.5 billion.

These measures allowed the system to continue operating without imploding, but at the expense of trust and security, because the assurance provided could be more or less useless. The break of the whole system, therefore, has only been postponed.

Interest in a debt-based monetary system

As you just realized, creating new money in a debt-based monetary system always requires someone to take on a new debt. But any debt not only needs to be paid in the future, but also requires an interest payment on the initial loan.

Since interest has to be paid also in the form of money, this situation creates an insoluble problem: when money is created by someone who takes on debts, only the exact amount of money equal to the loan is created.

When the loan is paid, additional money is required to pay interest.

Certainly, there is other money in circulation than just the money of this loan and the person who owes the loan could work to earn the money and thus pay off their loan and interest.

But if you take a look at the whole system, including all the money in circulation, then ALL the money in circulation exists because somewhere someone has accepted a loan and this loan needs to be paid with interest.

Therefore, it should be clear that there is always a lack of money in the system equal to the interest required for all loans issued.

Due to the overlapping of the various credit periods, this problem is not directly visible, but if all loans in the world had to pay back on a specific day, it would be obvious that only loans could be paid, but there would be no money to pay interest.

Thus, in a debt-based monetary system, the amount of money in circulation is forced to grow indefinitely due to the interest mechanism.

The additional money required to pay interest must be created by issuing new loans to someone. If individuals and private companies decide not to take on new debts, then there is only one credit recipient of last resort: the government.

Thus, the government needs to constantly increase the amount of the national debt to inject new money into the system. At this point, it should be clear that any political rhetoric about "putting a limit on the government's new debt" is useless.

The government has to become increasingly indebted and pay the national debt, this is IMPOSSIBLE.

There is not enough money in circulation to pay the entire national debt plus interest and any payment of public debt without instantly creating a new debt and withdrawing money from the system.

The amount of money in circulation has to grow constantly.

That's the reason why almost every time a government bonus is issued is due to the money needed to pay this loan and is simply created by issuing a new government title and using the money from the new title to pay the old bond that is due.

After all, a debt-based monetary system is a Ponzi scheme legalized by the government and will come to an end just like any other Ponzi scheme eventually that has come to an end.

National bankruptcy and monetary reform

The term national bankruptcy describes the situation in which the government of one country cannot meet its payment obligations – in other words, they run out of money.

This can only happen if the government fails to raise money through taxes or issue new government bonds. Issuing government bonds becomes increasingly difficult if potential buyers lose faith in the government's ability to pay their debts. In this case, only the central bank can help by making use of its monopoly to create money from nothing in exchange for receiving government bonds.

This process of converting government bonds into new money is also called "monetization" of government bonds.

Because monetization of government bonds causes an increase in the amount of money in circulation, the money that was in circulation before this monetization loses some of its value – especially if large amounts of government bonds are monetized. This loss in purchasing power is also referred to as inflation.

Within a debt-based monetary system, there is no limit to the amount of money that the central bank can create.

Thus, this process usually causes hyperinflation, which implies that money quickly loses its purchasing power. The term hyperinflation is generally used if the inflation rate exceeds 50% per month or – due to the effect of compound interest – 13000% per year.

Hyperinflation causes a flight to real assets, by exp. precious metals, which do not lose a large amount of their value during hyperinflation.

This is a list of countries that have experienced hyperinflation in the recent past. Typically, this is not a topic covered by mass media because it is very explosive: Austria, Hungary and Poland (1921-1924), Greece (1943/44), People's Republic of China (1949/50), Bolivia (1985), Nicaragua and Yugoslavia (1988), Brazil and Argentina (1989/90), Russia (1992), Georgia (1992-1994), Angola (1994-1997) and Zimbabwe (2006-2009).

Hyperinflation usually ends with monetary reform.

During a monetary reform, the old currency becomes virtually useless and replaced by a new currency.

In this process, different conversion rates apply to cash, deposits and debts. National bankruptcy is the main cause of monetary reform. Government bonds are generally more devalued than all other forms of debt.

The government, corporations and sectors of the population are treated unequally in this process.

I hope this has helped you understand more about the existing monetary system. Even if politicians and experts keep telling us that "money is safe," you may have understood that this is just the case as long as most of the population still has faith in their currency.

It is part of the work of politicians and experts to maintain this illusion of reliability and they are acting on behalf of the system lying to their own population.

However, the life expectancy of any debt-based monetary system is limited. So let me conclude this with an appropriate quote from Voltaire:

"The paper money eventually returns to its intrinsic value: zero" Voltaire (1694-1778)

If this book was a bit boring for you, I recommend you watch the animated movie "The American Dream".

It is a documentary disguised as animated short film and offers an excellent overview of how money works, as well as the history of the Federal Reserve System.

The address for this documentary is available in the quotes section. If you have trouble believing in some of the information you just read, it is recommended to check out a German Bundesbank publication in which the process of creating money "from nothing" is explicitly explicit.

Unfortunately, this publication is only available in German, but the most important passages have been translated into English.

Although it has begun this chapter with a historical view of how a gold-based monetary system has switched to a debt-based monetary system, I don't see the return to a gold standard as a viable "easy" solution.

If I was aware of a good solution, I would have mentioned here, but I haven't found a real solution that seemed convincing to me.

In order to achieve any human and realistic consensus, we first need more awareness and understanding within the population about the systemic failures in the current system and the research I did was to raise this necessary awareness.

While all Central Banks say gold is not money for obvious reasons, everyone holds tons of it, and Russia and China are two nations that are increasing their holdings, while Germany is repatriating the NY Fed, Venezuela repatriating the due to their economic ruin that is rapidly approaching.

After I found out how the monetary system works, I've been trying to educate others. I'm often seen as a conspiracy fanatic and people tend not to believe what I'm saying. Most of them have their own theory about how everything works and absolutely refuse to believe otherwise.

Over the years, I've learned that it's not worth hitting head-on with other people's opinions, because we all have our prospects and often want what seems to us to be the safest. I'm not saying with that I won't keep talking, if you ask me clearly, what my opinion is on the subject, I will have my most sincere answer bluntly without embellishments.

Chapter 4 :
Following digital money

Like a chain, money flows, circulates, and is liquid.

In fact, English law considers currency to be one of the main attributes of money.

But new virtual forms of money, such as bitcoin, should enjoy currency status?

The issue is far from resolved. Simon Gleeson, a partner at law firm Clifford Chance, explains why these definitions are important.

"Currency is simply another word for trading," Gleeson writes in his new book called ***Legal Concept of Money.***

"It was initially an attribute of physical currencies, and referred to the fact that money transfer is out of the application of the rule that nemo dat quod non habet."

Nemo dat quod non habet (in Portuguese, "you can't give what you don't have") is the legal principle that a thief can't pass or resell stolen property as if it were yours.

Instead, the original owner can retrieve it from a third party. The act of spending turns stolen banknotes and coins into currency.

But that rule doesn't extend to money. In his book, Gleeson explains how the exemption *nemo* of money works.

"When a thief spends stolen notes and coins, the recipient (the person who receives the payment) receives a good title of those notes, regardless of whether the person who transferred them has none," he says.

"If a thief steals five 10-pound bills from his wallet and you immediately seize it and can identify the specific notes, the £10 bills are still yours," Gleeson says.

"But if he can get to a store and spend them before you pick him up, you won't be able to get them back from the shopkeeper," he explains. Despite receiving stolen money, the shopkeeper also likes protection.

"The person who accepts the notes has the right to rely on the legal presumption that the money owner is the true rightful owner," Gleeson adds.

But if the currency law seems like an open invitation to theft and money laundering, there are restrictions.

For the money to pass in currency, there are two additional caveats: it needs to be exchanged for some form of value and must change hands in good faith. So a gift from the stolen money thief wouldn't turn it into currency.

And if the shopkeeper knew the pounds were stolen, he'd have to give them to the original owner.

These exemptions from the normal rules governing ownership may seem surprising. But it's easy to understand why they entered English law several hundred years ago.

If all notes and coins were subject to the claim of their original owners, whether one, ten or a hundred transactions in time, legal proceedings could multiply and trade would be paralysed.

But the distinction between money – a type of property with privileged legal status – and other forms of non-monetary property is difficult. And it's a topic that gained renewed urgency as a result of the invention of decentralized virtual money like bitcoin.

Money has no earmark

One of the reasons it makes no sense to try to keep up with money through a series of past transactions is that, in contrast to a stolen imaginary pig, money has no "trademark".

In other words, you cannot differentiate one note or currency from another as a result of your previous history. But what if money could be booked, say, digitally?

In fact, that's exactly what blockchain underlying digital assets, such as bitcoin, offer. If you open a software application such as bitcoin block explorer, you'll find a transparent record of transactions in the currency from the beginning.

Let's say you used stolen bitcoin, or bitcoin that had been used in a past drug business, to buy products from a shopkeeper.

We must not forget the exemption from money responsibility and rely on the inherent traceability of digital assets to try to capture crooks, say, linking the identity of those who carry out past transactions with some factors in the Real world?

Given blockchain status as a new form of public record, it's not surprising that some seek to divide digital assets into "clean" and "contaminated" currency units. For example, a group of researchers at the University of Cambridge says it proposes to make bitcoin legal – to give it money status – separating outstanding currencies into good and bad cuts, and treating only the first as currency.

Virtual currency can always be tracked, but notes can also. But this approach may not have the law on your side, says Clifford Chance's Gleeson.

"There is an argument that you can't treat the virtual currency as currency, since it can always be tracked," he writes in the Legal Concept of Money.

"The difficulty with this argument is that the same goes for the notes. Each banknote (in the UK and many other countries) has a unique identification number that, in theory, allows it to be tracked. "

What about the traceability inherent in blockchain?

In theory, at least, a distributed ledger could be used, unlike the serial number of a note, to show which hands the money had passed.

Gleeson also hits that.

"This (argument) is wrong for two important reasons," he says:

"First, no examination of the ledger can reveal whether the transferee of a unit was a value buyer," he says, citing one of the conditions for money to earn exemption from *nemo dat* rule.

"Where money is found in a person's hands," he continues, "it is assumed that it has been negotiated with him for value, unless the opposite can be proven. This is as true for virtual currency units as for individually identifiable notes."

And Gleeson returns to the main structural feature of a distributed book, it has no parent entity.

Regulators' approach to digital assets remains uneven... The second problem is that the information that would be revealed to an omniscient party with full access to all relevant public and private keys is irrelevant if neither party exists," he writes.

These legal arguments are important, not least because the regulatory approach to digital assets, such as bitcoin, remains uneven.

Central bankers' criticisms of digital assets such as bitcoin often tend to focus on the perception of their lack of utility, not on their legal status.

However, there was also a dogmatic tone in the statements of the Bank for International Settlements and the European Central Bank. And securities and futures regulators preferred to label bitcoin as a symbol or commodity, not as money.

It is a human custom that eventually prevails.

But according to one of the UK's leading financial lawyers, there is no reason in principle that these new digital assets do not serve as currency.

Money is, after all, a social construction and is the human custom that eventually prevails.

In his book, Gleeson argues that regulators and lawyers should remember their limitations in dictating new rules for this emerging sector.

"Legal certainty should support social consensus, but it is a very bad tool for trying to create that consensus," he says.

Coins... Coins everywhere.

Today, more than 180 currencies are in 195 countries, highlighting the absence of a free market. Governments have restricted currency markets to maintain financial control, with laws and institutions inhibiting free-market monetary systems.

Restrictions include borders, legal tender laws, capital controls, state decrees, and landlord privileges, local control, local monopolies on violence, debt extinction laws, capital gains taxes, guarantees implicit redemption for banks, central banks and dozens of other artificial barriers, to defend lower currencies.

Citizens of countries like Venezuela fail to protect their wealth from hyperinflation caused by monetary policies and irresponsible capital controls.

They also have to accept the lower currency in exchange for goods and services, as more stable currencies, such as the dollar, are sold with significant premiums. Until recently, they had no choice to leave this system.

In a 1984 interview, Friedrich Hayek said: ***"I don't believe we'll have good money again before we take the thing out of the government's hands.***

We can't take it violently out of the hands of government; all we can do is somehow indirectly introducing something they can't stop."

And in the Free Market Monetary System, he noted that: ***"the government monopoly and the issuance of money not only deprived us of good money, but also deprived us of the only process by which we can find out what would be good money.***

We don't even know exactly what exact qualities we want... because we were never allowed to experiment with it. We were never given the opportunity to find out what the best kind of money would be."

During my research to write this book I came across several interesting searches and one of them you can just type in google Bitcoin: the experiment that allows experimentation...

In 2008, Satoshi Nakamoto proposed Bitcoin, a top-down control-free financial system. Bitcoin, *"a system for electronic transactions without relying on trust,"* was not created to fit existing government and financial systems.

Bitcoin is the experiment that allows experimentation.

Unlike any other money, bitcoin is borderless, without permission, censorship resistant and verifiable. In other words, bitcoin could be the "indirect path" that goes beyond prohibitive mechanisms and legacy financial institutions that restrict access to money.

Often called digital gold, bitcoin is scarce and unpredictable.

Given its digital nature, bitcoin is divisible, portable and invisible and, unlike gold, capable of supporting centralization threats.

Introduced by Vijay Boyapati and increased by Dan Held, evaluates bitcoin, gold and fiat as they try to play the various roles of money.

The rise of cryptoccurrences

Cryptocurrencies are money.

With the exception of some, "cryptophones" are money or money overshadowed by technological jargon.

As bitcoin evolved and was appreciated, other cryptocurrencies – or altcoins – flooded the market, many of them repeating their "fundamental design flaws" and "limited functionality."

Ten years after bitcoin began, for better or worse, 2,000 cryptocurrencies joined the movement. Unlike the nationalized money market that dominated the 20th century, cryptocurrencies exist in a competitive market.

Given their open source roots, they are subject to open and inexpensive experimentation. As Jörg Guido Hülsmann points out in monetary production ethics, "the only way to discover society's natural money is to allow people to freely associate and choose the best means of exchange among the available alternatives."

In the last century, gold has given markets a glimpse of advantages, if not all, as a value reserve, a model perhaps for cryptocurrencies.

The question this time is how permanent this phenomenon will be.

Can Bitcoin become a new global currency?

Created in 2007, the world's first decentralized currency is now a form of accepted payment in dozens of countries around the world.

As more countries begin to adopt this innovative technology, it is clear that Bitcoin has the potential to become the new global currency not linked to a specific country or central bank. Many wondered if bitcoin could be the next global currency.

Although you may have heard the bitcoin term, it is understandable if you are still confused by the details of this digital payment system.

Before trying to answer the above question, it is important for me to understand exactly what a bitcoin is.

Bitcoin is a relatively new technology; in fact, it's less than a decade old.

As of autumn 2016, it is now a form of accepted payment in dozens of countries around the world. As more nations continue to adopt this innovative technology, the chances of bitcoin actually becoming the next global form of currency and one of the few that are not linked to the economy of a specific nation or a banking system.

Experts estimated that in just three years, by the year 2019, there would be five million active bitcoin users. Of these five million, 51% of users should stay out of the United States.

These are impressive statistics; however, consider an even more impressive estimate: bitcoins are expected to be the sixth largest reserve currency in the world by 2030.

That said, just as currency and exchange rate fluctuate constantly depending on external factors such as politics, current economic conditions, stock market trading and various transaction trends, bitcoins react similarly.

So far this year (2019), bitcoin has reached a market high of $4000 and a market low of $3000.

Mining blocks

Mining is another aspect of bitcoin operations and transactions that it is imperative to understand. To simplify a complicated process, understand that mining is – in essence – a record keeping service. The "Miners" ensure that a bitcoin chain is consistent, complete and unable to be tampered with.

To achieve this, miners repeatedly check and collect new transactions in a new existing transaction group called block.

It can help think so: miners insert transaction data into a powerful computer that essentially processes a seemingly endless sequence of calculations that increase in difficulty over time.

In January, Coin telegraph reported that 80% of bitcoin's entire offer, or 16.8 million Bitcoins, had been extracted.

Bitcoin has a limit of 21 million units according to the protocol created by Satoshi Nakamoto, first mentioned in the 2008 white paper, as a way to introduce digital shortages to cryptocurrency.

This means that only 4.2 million Bitcoins, or 20%, were issued until the 21 million units' limit of the cryptocurrency is issued.

The possibility of bitcoin emerging as the new global currency becomes even more important when it is considered that China is currently pushing only for it – a new currency.

Due to the recent economic slowdown in the United States, the dollar understandably faltered. China would like to see a currency not directly linked to the U.S. dollar, its stock markets and its banks.

The European Union (or simply the EU, abbreviated) also comes into play here, as they recently suggested that virtual currencies – such as bitcoin – should remain exempt from many traditional taxes, including the infamous value-added tax.

Value added tax is an additional amount passed on the value of an article, increasing at each stage of the production or distribution of an object. Similar to good, old, cold and heavy money, this is a big boost to the eventual viability of bitcoin as a global currency.

Let's also consider for a moment how bitcoin can change the game of the typical banking system. Banking systems, although protected, are unfortunately quite vulnerable to hacking attempts or malicious phishing.

That said, banks are typically as we are required to complete most current transactions – from the smallest to the life-changing purchases: buying shampoo at the pharmacy to exchange funds for buying a new home.

A cryptocurrency (*which is sometimes called encrypted currency*) is a form of monetary exchange using encryption to securely protect virtual transactions and restrict the creation of additional currency units (*helps think of it as false virtual invoices).*

Cryptocurrencies are a subset of digital currencies and their encryption methods are always strengthening, which means transactions and money are more protected for hackers.

These programs are beginning to stabilize, which only makes bitcoin more powerful on its journey to the global currency.

Bitcoin pros and cons

While all this looks great, it is important to remember that there are good and bad aspects of any major monetary competitor or any large-scale process change.

Pros:

1. With a decentralized currency system, the government or banks have no ties to the currency. This can be useful if a nation is in crisis or experiences a far-reaching economic crisis (similar to the "Great Recession" in the United States).

2. Transactions arc typically tax-free and cheap. (Except in the United States where it was considered as property instead of currency)

3. Money is easy to transfer to locations all over the world. Actually, it doesn't take time.

4. Banks may not use bitcoins saved from an individual for their own investments. Again, this means that government-related economic depressions will not affect the value of a bitcoin. 5. Block chain technology is very successful in eliminating the need for intermediaries whose goal is to fill the transactional trust gap.

Cons:

1. Bitcoin and other crypto currencies are highly volatile. This means that the value of a bitcoin can fluctuate dramatically – and often there is no way to predict a fluctuation or explain why it may have occurred. (high of $20,000 reached on December 17, 2017.)

2. Because bitcoins are not linked to a centralized institution, government or bank, their prices can rise and fall dramatically. (Prices subsequently fell to $6,000 on February 6, 2018.)

3. Users can choose bitcoins to pay for illegal goods and services (illegal substances, firearms, etc.) through the "dark web" online, as bitcoins can be more difficult to track.

4. Bitcoins are currently saved in online virtual wallets. Although it took the skill and expertise of a talented hacker to access these virtual wallets, this can be done, and hacking has occurred in the past.

5. Many consumers have difficulty understanding bitcoin or its complicated blockchain.

Governments could very well act radically and ban any Bitcoin transaction – governments are not good and that's why they let you buy Bitcoins.

The difficulty in regulating and/or banning Bitcoin is that it makes dialogue open in several of these countries. A quick look at the countries where Bitcoin is strictly forbidden evokes the dictatorial character of governments.

Banning Bitcoin based on the impossibility of government taxation is an authoritarian act.

The ban requires regulating internet access, banning websites, buying rights and sales...

That is, it hurts several of the democratic precepts of a nation. Some governments adopt bitcoin bristling characteristics and adopt limitations on Bitcoin such as prohibiting the sale of tangible goods in exchange for cryptocurrencies in order to prevent Bitcoin by buying illegal goods.

It doesn't make much sense, since banning legal trade does not inhibit illegal trade.

In fact – **Here I open room for another opinion – Governments that use arguments such as protection from the financial system or financial integrity of the population are only afraid of tax evasion and money left on the table.**

Governments can also selectively regulate the sector, especially in relation to taxation. It is similar to the current approach of the United Kingdom and the European Union.

Bitcoin Regulation in the UK

Eu regulatory proposals followed broadly the approach adopted by the French government, which included the following proposals:

"In order for users not to remain 100% anonymous and in a way, undisputed for possible crimes, exchanges must require identity certification and address. Exchanges should publish a set of instructions for consumers and regulators regarding the taxation of virtual currencies. Exchanges should limit payments or transactions of very high volume, meeting some requirements, similar to the limits that are already in force in relation to cash transactions."

Regulate, at continental level, i.e. to what is required by the EU, any companies offering exchanges between encrypted currencies and fiduciary currencies. According to Steve Keen, head of the School of Economics, History and Politics at Kingston University in London, bitcoin regulation is inevitable.

He noted that the existence of a future market in Bitcoin means that there will probably be a drop in price due to the variety of positions that can be taken in Bitcoin.

He also suggested that there are possibilities that, without regulation, hard forks can be "forced" to users.

The futures market in Bitcoin brings greater link and analogy to the traditional financial market and its trading style, which means that what happens in other markets can affect the price of Bitcoin. However, across the industry there are several opinions and drivers for regulation.

For some, bitcoin regulation would add legitimacy to cryptocurrency. However, for others, Bitcoin is down on the list of priorities, as it is not an urgent problem.

In addition, the cryptocurrency industry itself opposes large-scale regulation that would negatively affect the decentralized nature of Bitcoin.

The other issue, as suggested above by the EU approach, is that regulators remain unsure about what or how to regulate. The suitability of the cryptocurrency sector to existing structures is likely to stifle the industry.

However, to create a new regulatory and tax structure purely for cryptocurrencies results in significant expenses with the taxpayer.

In the hype of 2017 Bitcoin was pertinent subject in any meeting with friends or family, I myself let myself get carried away by the hype without knowing for sure what it was about.

Bitcoin has become the watchword in the office and at home.

As a result, it has become almost inevitable that regulation, in some way or another, would happen. Now, in 2019, with crypto market stalls in general, big players bet on the death of Bitcoin and crypto market, so efforts and studies to regulate something stillborn would be in vain.

The spotlight is no longer facing Bitcoin as in 2017. However, the major issues that remain are the way such regulations will take and the effect they will have on industry.

Bitcoin regulation in 2019

Where is Bitcoin legal?

Although not officially legal in several countries, governments are discussing the issue in an open and positive way. Several government agencies have been instructed that all Bitcoin transactions need to be carried out only in legal terms.

List of countries where Bitcoin is not illegal.

I particularly prefer to use the term "where Bitcoin is not illegal" than the abbreviated form, "where Bitcoin is legal". The reason, it's a simple terminological confusion.

When we say that bitcoin is not illegal in such a place, one to think that there is no norm that prohibits it. If I say, where Bitcoin is legal, there is the presumption of regulations dealing with the matter.

Therefore, in the places below there is no rule prohibiting Bitcoin, which does not mean that there is broad understanding and legal acceptance – You can simply move into a legal clean.

List of countries accepting bitcoin

Alande Antigua islands and Barbuda Australia Austria Azerbaijan
Belarus Belgium Brazil Brunei
Darussalam Bulgaria

Canada Chile Congo Costa Rica Croatia Cuba Cyprus Czech Republic

Denmark Dominican Republic

Estonia Finland France Georgia

Germany Gibraltar Greece

Hong Kong Hungary

Iceland Iran Iraq Ireland

Man Island Israel Italy Japan Japan Jersey Kuwait Lebanon Liberland

Jamahiriya Arab Libya Libya

Liechtenstein Lithuania Luxembourg Malta Mexico Monaco Mongolia

Netherlands New Zealand Nicaragua Northern Mariana Islands

Norway Philippines Poland Portugal Puerto Rico Romania Fed. Russian San Marino Serbia Singapore Slovakia Slovenia

South Korea South Korea Spain Svalbard and Jan Mayen Sweden Switzerland Taiwan Thailand Peru Ukraine Uzbekistan EU America UK Sahara Western Zimbabwe

Can regulating Bitcoin bring security?

The incredible turnaround on the roller coaster and the fall in cryptocurrency prices in 2018 and the growing popularity of different types of cryptocurrencies have finally attracted the attention of regulators.

Here's the issue, though, Bitcoin is not centrally regulated by any government, so each government has its back on the issue.

Reports for tax purposes and regulating ICO's (initial coin offerings) are the first steps of an attempt... Even if the actual purchase and sale of cryptocurrencies with blockchain technology is extremely secure, humans are involved in negotiations, exchanges and initial offers.

That means fraud is already happening.

Bitcoin's new regulations have the power to change the cryptocurrency market.

But most analysts think bitcoin regulation will be positive – at least in the long run.

Let's take a look at what's happening now, and what might happen in the future. How Bitcoin regulations can change the market:

In the short term, regulations can suppress cryptocurrency trading values. In the long term, however, regulations, if made properly, are expected to stabilise the market and make it safer investment.

The SEC is seeking to regulate OICs as bonds and is cracking down on fraud. Bitcoin regulation has the potential to make the market much safer.

It will still be a risky investment, but with protections for investors it is less likely that the market will need to face so much external manipulation.

Overall, this is good for people who want to invest in cryptocurrencies. Safer markets mean confidence, which in turn reduces asset volatility, giving greater predictability to price and this is critical when we talk about a currency.

Have you ever wondered if the Dollar varied as much as Bitcoin?

At this time, regulators seem to be focusing on two specific areas. Investor taxation and Initial Currency Offerings (ICOs).

Capital gains from encrypted revenues are little reported in most countries, with an estimated 59% of people so denying gains in the United States – I think it's much more!

This is obviously an area of concern for tax authorities like the IRS. And the IRS is starting to act.

They collected 14,000 activity records from Coinbase (One of the most popular exchanges) – This means that the IRS is eyeing its earnings.

So if you win in the crypto markets, you might want to declare these gains before the IRS declares them to you – I don't advise this, Tax is theft, remember?

Bitcoin Tax

Another body concerned with regulation is the ICO. For you to understand for good, the ICO treats Bitcoin as bonds, while other agencies, such as the SEC, treat Bitcoin as securities.

That's why there's so much discussion about regulation.

Looks like regulators are trying to catch up.

What investors should know about regulation before buying Bitcoin?

Bitcoin can be very sexy, I confess that to me it seems quite attractive to me, but before making any investment, first we have to understand very well all the attractive faces of Bitcoin.

It's reminiscent of the early Days of the Internet, when everyone was pouring money into dot.com without even knowing what they meant in depth. Due to the volatile nature of cryptocurrency, it is important to understand its risk.

It's a good idea to ask if investing in bitcoin or other cryptocurrency is a good option for you and if you're ready to lose your money. That sounds hostile, but it's true.

Bitcoin is beautiful and wonderful. You can really get rich with Bitcoin. The odds are much higher than with your boring work.

Another reality, even more likely is that you are greedy and opportunistic and everything can be lost instantly through cybercrime or devaluation.

It's like a roller coaster: If you like adrenaline and have a high risk tolerance, then it might be a good idea to invest. Remember that the term "invest" here is being used freely. Cryptocurrencies are very speculative – just as a casino is speculative.

Does regulating Bitcoin affect the price?

Surprisingly the first steps of the Bitcoin regulation are not affecting quotes much. We've seen some falls when a new regulatory item comes out.

The great thing to remember about encryption is that it is risky, as regulators take action to put consumer protection into practice. The fact is, Bitcoin is not supported by any central government.

All seemingly small regulatory ads boosted the price of bitcoin and other crypts in 2018. On March 20, 2018, Argentine President Mauricio Macri spoke at the G-20 meeting in Buenos Aires, Argentina:

"At a G-20 meeting this month, the president of Argentina's central bank outlined a deadline for G20 members to submit "specific recommendations on what to do with the Bitcoin case" and said task forces are working to present proposals by July."

The leader of Italy's central bank told reporters after the meeting in Buenos Aires that cryptocurrencies pose risks but should not be banned, according to Reuters.

The Financial Stability Council, a global agency that manages the financial regulation of the G-20 economies, adopted a cautious tone in responding to requests from some countries to crack down on digital currencies.

"The initial assessment is that cryptographic assets pose no risks to global financial stability at this time," council

Chairman Mark Carney said in a letter on March 18.

Carney, who is also head of the Bank of England, pointed to the relatively small size of the asset class compared to the entire financial system. -***"Even at its recent peak, its combined global market value (Bitcoin) is less than 1% of global GDP."***

The International Monetary Fund also called for more cooperation.

IMF Managing Director Christine Lagarde highlighted the potential of cryptocurrency as a vehicle for money laundering and terrorist financing.

(That's what they think, but okay, we already know why...)

In a March blog post, Lagarde called for policies that protect consumers in the same way as the traditional financial sector.

Bitcoin, regulation and Japan

Japan is the largest bitcoin market. Almost half of the daily volume of the digital currency is traded in the country's currency, according to Cryptocompare data.

Last week, the agency issued a warning to Hong Kong-based Binance for operating in the country without a license. Hacks have been a problem in Japan and elsewhere.

Japan was the first country to adopt a national system to regulate cryptocurrency trading after its exchanges were subject to some well-known violations, including Mt. Gox.

In March, Japanese regulators issued punishment notices for several exchanges and forced some to completely disrupt business after the $530 million digital currency theft of Exchange Coincheck.

Bitcoin regulation and the United States

FinCen, an agency at the Treasury Department, said in 2013 that: "virtual currency has no legal course in any jurisdiction."

The U.S. deals with the second highest volume of bitcoin, about 26%, according to Cryptocompare.

U.S. regulators differ in their definitions of bitcoin and other cryptocurrencies.

The Securities and Exchange Commission has indicated that it sees the digital currency as a guarantee.

In early March, the agency expanded its scrutiny and said it is seeking to enforce securities laws for everything from cryptocurrency exchanges to digital asset storage companies known as wallets.

The agency focused on initial coin offerings, or digital currencies launched through fundraising, known as symbolic sales, and stepped up efforts to police them through recent subpoenas.

The Commodity Futures Trading Commission says bitcoin is a commodity. (CFTC)

The IRS says, "Cryptocurrency is not really a currency" and has issued guidance on how Bitcoin should be taxed.

Treasury Secretary Steven Mnuchin has said about bitcoin's ability to help criminals, telling CNBC in Davos in January that its main focus on cryptocurrencies is "to ensure that they are not used for illicit activities."

Bitcoin, regulation and Europe

No EU member state can introduce its own currency, according to European Central Bank President Mario Draghi. About 4% of the cryptocurrency's daily volume is made in euros, according to Cryptocompare.

EU leaders have expressed concern about money laundering. European Commission Vice-President Valdis Dombrovskis said at a February round table in Brussels that digital assets "pose risks related to money laundering and financing illicit activities."

Exchanges and E-Wallets should be under the "Money Laundering Prevention Directive," Dombrovski said.

"The committee will continue to monitor these markets in conjunction with other stakeholders at EU and international level, including the G-20."

Draghi rejected Estonia's attempt to create a state-backed cryptocurrency called "estcoin."

"No member state can introduce its own currency,"

Draghi said in September, - "The euro zone currency is the euro."

Regulations differ within the block. France's financial regulator, Autorite des Marches Financiers, released a list of 15 exchanges that would be blocked in March. The country said it will make a joint proposal with Germany to regulate the bitcoin cryptocurrency market, Reuters reported.

Bank of England Governor Mark Carney: "Only the pound sterling is legal currency in the UK."

Bitcoin exchanges and users are required to meet the same anti-money laundering standards against terrorism as other financial institutions, according to the BOE.

Exponential price gains in cryptocurrencies are "speculative mania," Carney said in early March.

"The time has come to maintain the encryption asset ecosystem to the same standards as the rest of the financial system," Carney said in a speech. "Being part of the financial system brings enormous privileges, but with great responsibilities."

Carney said the digital currency "has virtually failed so far" in the traditional aspects of money." It's not a value reserve because it's all over the map. Nobody uses it as a means of trading."

Many virtual currencies are trying to dislodge the British pound, but "only the pound sterling is legal currency in the UK," Carney said in another March speech.

The Financial Conduct Authority called cryptographic assets "high-risk speculative products" in a warning to consumers in November 2018.

Bitcoin, regulations and South Korea

Bitcoin exchange policy is legal, but the use of anonymous bank accounts for virtual currency trading is prohibited. You need to register with the South Korean Financial Services Commission.

Trading in South Korea accounts for about 4% of the daily volume of bitcoin.

For other cryptocurrencies, such as XRP, trading in the Korean won requires a premium for U.S. dollars.

Asia's fourth largest economyse has become a trade hub, but regulators have given mixed signals.

Financial authorities said in 2013 that bitcoin and other digital currencies are not legitimate currencies, according to the Korea Herald.

South Korea's justice minister said in January that the government is considering stopping cryptocurrency exchanges.

A petition calling on the government to contain "irrational" regulation received 280,000 signatures after the announcement.

The government responded by saying it will take firm action against illegal and unfair acts in cryptocurrency trading.

Last year, the Financial Services Commission banned local financial companies from trading Bitcoin futures, according to local publication Business Korea.

The commission also banned the use of anonymous bank accounts for trading since January 2018, but said it does not intend to completely close domestic exchanges. The government said that while it does not prohibit Bitcoin exchanges, initial currency offerings and futures contracts will remain under scrutiny.

At the end of February, a government official said South Korea had not yet decided how to regulate.

"The government has not yet come to any conclusion. Sufficient consultations should come first," Hong Nam-ki, the government's policy coordination minister, told parliament.

Bitcoin, Regulation and China

Trading bitcoin in China is technically illegal. In 2017, the government banned start-up companies from raising funds by selling new digital currencies – and closed cryptocurrency exchanges.

In January, a Chinese central banker said authorities should ban the trade in virtual currencies as well as individuals and companies that provide related services. But encryption activity continued through alternative channels such as mining.

Chinese authorities are trying to end the practice, according to Reuters, which cited an internal memo from a government meeting in January. India is taking steps to make encrypted currencies illegal in its payment system and is seeking to appoint a regulator to oversee exchanges.

The government "will take all measures to eliminate the use of these cryptographic resources in financing illegitimate activities or as part of the payment system," India's finance minister told lawmakers in New Delhi in February this year, according to a transcript of The Hindu newspaper.

The country's tax department sent warnings about cryptocurrency investment to tens of thousands of citizens after a national survey showed that more than $3.5 billion in transactions were made in a 17-month period.

Bitcoin, regulation and Switzerland

Swiss regulators have earned the reputation of some of the worlds friendliest when it comes to cryptocurrency.

Four out of 10 of the largest proposals for initial coin offerings were based in Switzerland, according to a PwC report.

The town of Zug, south of Zurich, is nicknamed "Crypto Valley" and houses several block companies such as the Ethereum Foundation and card and cryptocurrency company Cardano.

PwC's report highlighted how the small Swiss municipality emerged as a "focus for blockchain-based companies and consulting services" and the growing "reputation of being a welcoming environment for companies and technology companies."

The Swiss Financial Market Supervisory Authority has established clear guidelines for OICs.

Economy Minister Johann Schneider-Ammann told reporters in January that he wants the country to become "cryptographic," the Financial Times reported. Swiss National Bank President Thomas Jordan said in September 2018 that he sees bitcoin as more of an investment than a currency.

How can we analyse has countries that prohibit Bitcoin, those that legalize Bitcoin and those that do not deal with the subject, example of Ecuador and China, where Bitcoin is expressly prohibited — The United States, which rely on permissive regulation —and those that do not have specific regulation, such as Brazil.

The only regulatory/legal framework that is being processed in congress is bill 2303/2015.

This bill is not, however, a regulatory instrument... It aims to include virtual currencies and air mileage programs in the category of payment arrangements, under the supervision of the Central Bank.

It seems kind of wrong to put bitcoin and mileage programs in the same drawer as airlines, but okay!!

So, if the non-regulation under the subject, playing with the Federal Constitution of 1988 under the arm, where: "No one is obliged to do or fail to do something, but by virtue of law." – **You are not obliged to collect taxes on the CIRCULATION of Bitcoin or Altcoins.**

The Federal Government does not see Bitcoin as money. There are, however, those who argue that ICMS (tax on the movement of goods and services) on the operation of buying

Bitcoin in exchanges should be addressed. Different is the case, and there is nothing to talk about incidence of ICMS when the transaction is performed via P2P.

In the case of the ISS (tax on services of any nature) there are those who defend the tax on any payment for service provision made by Bitcoin.

Of course, the IRS vampires didn't lose the mouth of Bitcoin.

"Under the regulatory framework, digital currencies should be reported as other assets in the Income Tax Statement." preaches the Brazilian Internal Revenue Service, but in Portugal still nothing, for now.

The fact is, you don't need it and you shouldn't declare your coins. The government does not have access to its "wallet" and that is why Bitcoin and Altcoins will be up to the rulers... they need to rely on the stupidity of the taxpayer to rip out their sweaty money.

I look forward to a very excited tone to treat this chapter, my will was to sum up all this bla-bla-bla in **-Tax is theft and Bitcoin is the ultimate of liberalism!**

Chapter 5 :

Conclusion...

There's still a lot of cloth for the sleeve. We will certainly have incessant new chapters in this novel about regulation.

The next chapters, is that they can really completely change the direction (*and prices*) of Bitcoin and altcoins and the resolution of the SEC and the Bitcoin ETF.

In my view Bitcoin has a beautiful path ahead of me. Bitcoin won't die and it won't turn into dust, rest assured!

If the future of this path requires regulation, I don't know – I'd like it not – but denying the strong tendency to this strand is stupid.

And as I said before:

Bitcoin is the evolutionary maxim of liberalism...

To what extent is this maxim confused in the tenuous line of anarchism? - I don't know, but it's time to review the whole system and as I mentioned at the beginning of the book, just embellishments when it comes to talking about money, it's time to be realistic and carefully analyse all the "cards" that are on the table…

In the existing financial system, currency creation is monopolized by central banks printing money under the supervision of "professional" economists.

Journalism professor David S. Allen (2005) explains how science has become a methodology that underpins professional legitimacy.

Specialized knowledge and professionalism depend heavily on the so-called creed of objectivity. This creed is the dominant logic based on a positivist and empiric epistemology accepted by scientists and experts in many fields.

He claims impartiality to researchers as if they were free from their own agendas and prejudices, when, in reality, as one of the founders of sociology Max Weber pointed out, the value-free objectivity of researchers is simply impossible.

Under this claim of objectivity, the prejudices and subjective interests of the elite go beyond democratic consensus and are codified directly in monetary policy.

This is a pseudoscience of the economy that closes the feedback system and has so far helped escape the critical examination.

It creates mathematics that is divorced from the reality of people's needs and is used to enact the current pyramid scheme of wealth redistribution of the pyramid from the bottom up.

Digital numbers on computers can become abstractions that tend to divert the flow of real work or stagnate real economic activity. This manipulated book deprives the power of ordinary people to work creatively with numbers that represent their true value.

These numbers have become weapons of mass deception to enslave people through debt, usury and devaluation through quantitative easing.

It is this understanding that allows us to continue talking about money as if it were a limited resource like bauxite or oil, to say "there is simply not enough money" to fund social programs, to talk about the immorality of public debt or public spending, "expelling" the private sector.

What the Bank of England has admitted is that none of this is really true. To quote their own initial summary: "Instead of banks receiving deposits when families save and lend them, bank loans create deposits"... "In normal times, the central bank does not set the amount of money in circulation, nor is bank money "multiplied" in more loans and deposits."

In other words, all we know is not just wrong – it's backwards. When banks make loans, they make money. This is because money is really just an IOU.

The role of the central bank is to preside over a legal order that effectively grants banks the exclusive right to create promissory notes of a certain kind, which the government will recognize as legal currency by its willingness to accept them in paying taxes.

There's really no limit on how much banks could create, as long as they can find someone willing to borrow.

They will never be caught red-handed, for the simple reason that borrowers usually do not take the money and put it under the mattress; ultimately, any money from a bank loan will end up back at some bank again.

Thus, for the banking system as a whole, the whole loan becomes another deposit.

What's more, to the extent that banks need to buy funds from the central bank, they can borrow as much as they want; all you really do is set the interest rate, the cost of money, not your amount. Since the beginning of the recession, central banks in the U.S. and England have reduced that cost to almost nothing.

In fact, with "quantitative easing", they are effectively pumping as much money as they can for banks without producing any inflationary effect.

What this means is that the real limit on the amount of money in circulation is not how much the central bank is willing to lend, but how much the government, firms and ordinary citizens are willing to borrow.

Government spending is the main driver of all this (newspapers admit, if you read carefully, that the central bank finances the government in the end). Therefore, there is no doubt that public spending "expels" private investment. It's exactly the opposite.

Why did the Bank of England suddenly admit all this? Well, one reason is because it's obviously true. The Bank's job is to actually run the system and lately the system is not working especially well.

It is possible that she has decided that keeping the fantasy version of the economy that proved to be so convenient for the rich is simply a luxury that she can no longer afford.

But politically, this is taking a huge risk. Just consider what could happen if mortgage holders realized the money borrowed by the bank is not actually the life savings of some economic pensioner, but something the bank has just created through its possession of a magic wand that we, the public, deliver to that end.

Control of ***OUR money*** allowed these criminals to purchase our political systems and our industries, from education and law to food, defence and medicine.

This hole is very deep and full of slime! Essentially, in my youth I've always been told that bankers are much smarter than us and that by depositing our money into their banks, they can work with financial sorcery to make money and pay us interest dividends.

This is still being taught in our teaching systems and is completely an absolute waste. Worse than that, nowadays we can't do anything without having a bank account, we're completely dependent.

Money has always been one of the main techniques used to control humanity.

The other medium was traditionally religion, but now we also have laws, education, medicine, media and food.

These are the main factors that enslave us. The true origins of money have been potentially lost in the mists of time, but what is clear is that our monetary systems have always been manipulated.

I often wonder who gave this knowledge of money and its manipulation to humans, and why – but that's a topic I leave for another book!

Although I have always considered myself a spiritual person, I do not adopt any particular religion. I read all the major religious works and during my reading of the Bible I came across an interesting story.

Jesus is always described as a peaceful person, but there is a single account of Jesus losing patience and resorting to an act of violence... Jesus was Jewish and, when he visited the temple during Easter, he was outraged to see trade and exchange of money inside the temple.

Although this was not illegal and provided a service to the Jewish people, there were allegations of corruption and speculation.

"And, entering the temple of God, he cast out all who sold and bought in the temple; and he knocked down the tables of the changers and the chairs of those who sold doves, and said to them: It is written: house will be called a house of prayer, but you made a lair of thieves. "-Matthew 21: 12–13

If you believe this story is true or just an allegory, it's interesting to note that our fight against the powers of money is thousands of years old!

Banks are allowed to create money out of nowhere and the fact that they have the "knife and cheese" to lend it to us with interest, confuse the mind!

This is a sad reflection of our lack of education. This is basically a legalized fraud and was initiated by the goldsmiths. Reviewing what I wrote at the beginning of this book, we can not forget one of the most famous families of gold smithing that history has ever known...

The Rothschild Family – Owners of central banks!

The Federal Reserve is not owned by the United States government and has no reservations.

It has often been said that the Federal Reserve is like Federal Express.

As is often the case, your name is a clever mistake to confuse the public.

The current Federal Reserve is the third version of a central bank in the United States and the history of this version is totally fascinating.

The Federal Reserve has the only monopoly on currency printing in the United States. When the government needs currency they go to the Federal Reserve, which prints the currency.

There are several reasons for this, but one obvious one is raising the currency for wars knowing that the American people would not accept taxes.

The Federal Reserve prints this currency and lends it to the government (the people).

The cost of this process is small.

The total value of the currency is now owned by the government (the people) to the Federal Reserve.

As if that wasn't enough, they also want to charge interest on that principle. This interest cannot be paid in gold, euros, coffee beans or hugs.

Must be paid in U.S. dollars. These dollars never existed because they were never printed and people have been in debt and can never break free.

We just have a lot to think about here, right?

THE BASIC FRACTIONAL RESERVE BANKING CYCLE

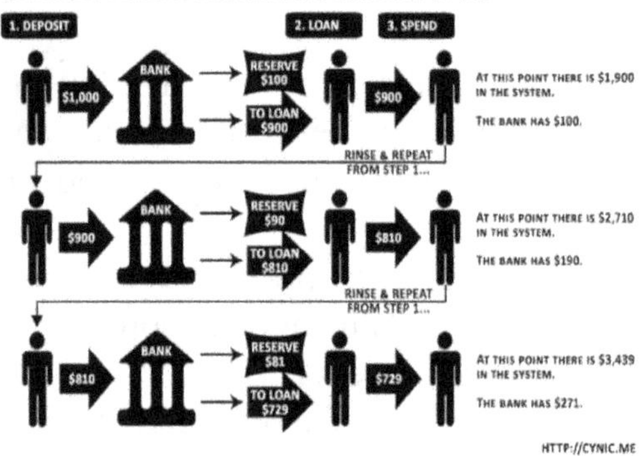

Visual explanation of the basic fractional reserve banking cycle.

This is a terrible situation instigated by the global banking elite, but the problem does not end there.

There is still a more insidious tax imposed on the people that hurt the poorest people in our economies.

This is the hidden tax on inflation. We've all heard of inflation, but few people seem to be able to explain it. Inflation is the reduction of the purchasing power of our currency when the currency supply is increased. It is estimated that since the Federal Reserve was created in 1913, the U.S. dollar was devalued by more than 96%!

The greatest damage caused by this sad process is reserved for the poorest people! Conversely, the biggest winners of this situation are the big corporations and banks that have access to that money before it reduces to the economy and increases inflation.

It is important to note that the Federal Reserve has never been audited publicly, so it is really impossible for us to define how financial chicanism happened!

One of the lonely voices that continually request an audit was Ron Paul. The truth is that money belongs to the people and they have the innate right to manage it.

Although this is not an opinion shared by the global banks that run our planet!

It is estimated that in 2000 there were seven countries without a global banker owned or controlled by the Central Bank, it is worth knowing: Afghanistan, Iraq, Sudan, Libya, Cuba, North Korea and Iran.

Today there are perhaps four left: Sudan, Cuba, North Korea and Iran.

It's no coincidence that these countries are demonized by the corporate media controlled by bankers, or that they have even been attacked with crazy wars from which we always go out without realizing why.

My prediction is that there will be continued pressure to use U.S. military power to invade and subdue these countries until the entire planet is owned and controlled by these global avaristic bankers. As usual, this will be paid by the U.S. population through inflation and blood.

Thinking of all the millions of poor people who have to lose their lives, families and homes to achieve that goal breaks my heart. Perhaps, as more of us become aware of this situation, we can make changes before its too late!

Let's see once again how this small group of global bankers managed to create money out of nowhere and lend it to us with interest, they were able to buy and control almost every aspect of our lives.

They possess our traitorous politicians, our extinct educational system, poisonous medical system and our nasty food production.

They control our military and security services. They also direct our means and legal systems. That's why I'm writing this book.

The truth is that bankers have almost everything and, through their actions, show a complete disregard for human life and the health of our planet. Because they can print as much money as they want – it's not money they covet.

They just seem to worry about control and power. What is important to remember is that they are manipulating every aspect of our lives and it all starts with control of our monetary system. Once we understand this, many events take on a new light and begin to fit into a comprehensive agenda.

Don't believe what the system tells you.

Do your own research and keep your eyes open!

Remember that money is illusory! Then educate the people around you!

The question no one seems to ask is, who is this debt for? Online research has provided me with some complex answers, but the truth is that this money is due to the global bankers who created it out of nowhere.

So, what can we do about it?

The first thing to do is educate us and I hope this book has been informative and useful for this process!

As I promised myself, I will continue to discuss this matter and educate everyone I know, especially my children, because I want them to have access to the knowledge I never had during my youth.

The second process we must undertake is to initiate action. The protests are good, but they don't seem to be very effective – we need to do more and I'd love to hear your thoughts about the appropriate actions we can take!

In the Notes of this book, I leave my email directly; feel free to send me your ideas, because I believe that together we make a difference.

Another approach is to engage with systems beyond the reach of global bankers.

Grow your own food and exchange it with your friends, trade, learn natural healing, and of course use crypto coins.

I have my suspicions that global bankers are trying to manipulate the crypto currency economy through legislation and bottlenecks like exchanges...

Right now I'm looking for a decentralized trading platform that is community property! My criticism of our banking system is not level for all bankers.

Most are just doing mundane jobs pushing paper without any knowledge of the blows and misery that are involved in their perpetuation. I have several good friends who are involved in banking in Portugal and England and they are amazing people with young families who don't realize who they actually work for.

Through education, action and development of decentralized systems, we can begin to get out of this miserable situation.

I have a lot of hope for humanity and believe that we will be able to achieve the necessary changes to remove these leeches.

This was a long book, and I wonder how many of you will read!

I just scratched the surface of this fascinating and dense subject, but the information I wanted to leave to my children and the future generation is all compiled in this research of mine. I finish this book with a fascinating message from a great woman...

"I freed a thousand slaves and could have freed a thousand more if they knew they were slaves."
- Harriet Tubman

THE END

Notes

Carla Frederico

Email: div3rgentmotivation@gmail.com

QUOTES

Mr Graeber. Debt: the first 5,000 years. 2011, Melville House Publishing.

J. Baron. Making changes: use of currency and social transformation among classic Mayans. Annual meeting of the Society for American Archaeology, Washington, D.C., April 13, 2018.

S. Fitzpatrick. Banking on stone money: the influence of traditional "coins" on blockchain technology. Annual meeting of the Society for American Archaeology, Washington, D.C., April 13, 2018.

L. Gamble. Origin and use of shell bills money in Southern California. Annual meeting of the Society for American Archaeology, Washington, D.C., April 13, 2018.

S. Hutson Creations of the Lord: slavery and sacrifice of the New World. Annual meeting of the Society for American Archaeology, Washington, D.C., April 13, 2018.

S. Kowalewski. Economic institutions in ancient Greece and Meso-America. Annual meeting of the Society for American Archaeology, Washington, D.C., April 13, 2018.

R. Rosenswig. Is the study of old money really so difficult? Annual meeting of the Society for American Archaeology, Washington, D.C., April 13, 2018.

The American Dream – Documentary https://www.youtube.com/watch?v=VB7raTsZ9qs

www.ingramcontent.com/pod-product-compliance
Lightning Source LLC
Chambersburg PA
CBHW060019210326
41520CB00009B/937

* 9 7 8 0 2 4 4 5 4 0 5 2 4 *